Start to Finish

Developmentally Sequenced Fine Motor Activities

for Preschool Children

Start to Finish

Developmentally Sequenced Fine Motor Activities for Preschool Children

by

Nory Marsh, M.Ed., OTR

imaginart

Bisbee, Arizona

Imaginart International, Inc.
307 Arizona Street
Bisbee, AZ 85603
Phone: (800) 828-1376
            (520) 432-5741
Fax: (800) 737-1376
            (520) 432-5134

Edited by Kirsteen E. Anderson.

Illustrated by Deborah Nore and Ruth Bush.

Cover by Bill Benoit and Deborah Nore.

ISBN 1-883315-29-8

Manufactured in the U.S.A.

Contents

Acknowledgments

For the Lord gives wisdom, and from his mouth come knowledge and understanding.

(Proverbs 2:6 NIV)

The activities and concepts presented in this manual are a compilation of personal experience and wisdom I have gained from numerous sources, both published and unpublished. I am indebted to many authors, therapists and teachers who have offered insights, inspiration and leadership into the complexities of fine motor development and the acquisition of fine motor skills during the preschool years.

In addition, I would like to thank my husband, David, for his inspiration and support, without which I could not have completed this curriculum, and all Regis University staff who aided in the completion of this project, especially Gary Upton and Sharon Sweet.

~Nory Marsh

Introduction

Start to Finish is a comprehensive course of activities for remediating fine motor delays in preschoolers (ages three to five years). This program may be implemented with older children whose fine motor skills fall in the three- to five-year range, with modifications to the activities if necessary to ensure they are socially and cognitively appropriate to the child's chronological age.

The materials are designed so that they can be implemented either directly by an occupational therapist (OT) or by a variety of other adults—including certified occupational therapy assistants (COTAs), parents, teachers and teacher's aides—in consultation with an occupational therapist (OT). They can be implemented in a variety of settings, such as in an integrated preschool, at home with a parent or in pull-out therapy with an OT or COTA. A significant benefit of this program is that it enables children to receive appropriate, developmentally sequenced practice in fine motor skills with a reduced amount of direct occupational therapy services. Before these activities are used with a child, he or she must receive a comprehensive occupational therapy evaluation to ensure that the activities are appropriate and to determine the level at which to begin. The occupational therapist also plays an instrumental role in supervising the implementation of this program and children's progress in it.

Success in academic tasks such as handwriting and cutting requires proficiency in several fine motor skills. Many preschool children with mild to moderate fine motor delays have good language and social skills and generally function well in the preschool setting. As a result, their delay is easily overlooked during daily interactions. It has been my experience that these children actively avoid fine motor activities because they find them difficult. The resulting lack of practice may widen the gaps in their fine motor ability. Then, when they enter elementary school and face more intense fine motor demands (e.g., handwriting), they often fail to perform to their potential simply because they lack the skills to meet these demands. According to Wessel (1988), "many educators consider the development of fine motor skills to be an important goal in the primary curriculum" (p. 5), and the "mastery of fine motor skills is more closely related to school achievement than standard intelligence test scores" (p. 9). Therefore, it is critical that children with fine motor delays be identified during preschool and that they receive practice in the fine motor skills that are prerequisite to cutting, pasting, coloring, beginning writing and other tasks in the elementary school classroom.

Miller and Brizzell (1983, cited in Wessel, 1988) suggested that programs emphasizing development of fine motor skills will better prepare children for formal learning. *Start to Finish* is a developmentally sequenced program that addresses the specific fine motor skills children with mild to moderate fine motor delays struggle with, and prepares them to tackle such classroom activities with confidence and success.

Program Overview

Start to Finish consists of a total of 70 fine motor activities that target skills normally acquired between ages three and five years. Each activity requires between 10 and 30 minutes to complete, depending on each child's level of independence and speed. The activities were selected to be age appropriate, developmentally sequenced and enjoyable for children. They are designed to break down the process of fine motor development into small increments that most children can easily manage. In addition, they require minimal preparation time and use readily available materials.

The activities should be conducted in the order presented in this manual, without skipping any, unless an occupational therapist advises otherwise for a particular child. The activities are carefully organized in developmental sequence to ensure that children develop a foundation of basic skills before being presented with tasks that demand more advanced fine motor skills. This increases children's success and confidence because they are not asked to do fine motor tasks that they do not have the prerequisite skills for. It has been my experience in using these activities that presenting them in developmental sequence helps children learn the skills much more quickly and with much less frustration than if they are presented with activities far beyond their current skill level.

For the purposes of this program, fine motor skills will refer only to fine motor movements done with the hands. A *mild fine motor delay* is defined as a delay of between one month and one year, and a *moderate fine motor* delay is a delay of between one and two years. The presence and degree of fine motor delay should be determined by a trained examiner administering an appropriate standardized developmental assessment. In addition, an occupational therapist should evaluate children being considered for this program to determine what areas need to be addressed and the appropriateness of the program for individual children's needs. The fine motor areas specifically addressed within the program are in-hand manipulation skills, pencil grasp, scissors skills and grasp and visual motor skills for coloring and drawing. These skills will be described further in "Overview of Motor Development."

The program is divided into three units. **Unit 1** primarily targets in-hand manipulation because this area underlies the fine motor skills addressed later in the sequence of activities; early precutting and prewriting skills are addressed only briefly. The focus of **Unit 2** is on developing efficient pencil and scissors grasps, the initial stages for cutting skills and visual motor skills for coloring and prewriting. In **Unit 3**, the focus is on refining efficient pencil and scissors grasps and on more advanced cutting skills and visual motor skills for coloring and prewriting. Higher-level in-hand manipulation skills are included within both **Units 2 and 3**. It is recommended that children use markers, rather than crayons or pencils, for most prewriting and coloring activities, because markers are generally easier for children to use. (Note: Pencil grasp refers generically to grasping any writing implement.)

Individual students will master these skills at different rates. Some children may require repeated practice with early activities before they are ready to move on to more difficult ones. Extension activities for additional practice are suggested for every exercise. Because the activities in this manual span a two-year developmental range, children are very unlikely to complete the entire sequence within one year. This wide range of exercises is presented so that children at a variety of skill levels have tasks appropriate to their level. Children should begin the program with whatever activity is commensurate to their current skill level, as determined by an occupational therapist; they need not begin with Activity 1 if they have already progressed beyond this level.

The activities are ordered to reflect the typical sequence of fine motor development. However, it is not unusual for children to have gaps in specific areas of development or to demonstrate "splinter skills," isolated skills that are more advanced than their overall level of development. Thus you may find that a child struggles with early activities but can successfully complete certain later activities. In these instances consultation with an occupational therapist is advised. Children who have gaps only in specific areas may not need to complete all the tasks within the program. For example, a child who demonstrates good in-hand manipulation, but struggles with prewriting and scissors skills, may be able to skip all the activities that target primarily in-hand manipulation. Again, such recommendations should be made by an occupational therapist.

Each activity is numbered in developmental sequence. The activity description states the goal of the activity and the specific skill areas targeted. (Some skills that are prerequisite to but not directly targeted within the activity may not be listed.) Necessary supplies are listed, followed by instructions for completing the activity. Modifications and adaptations are suggested for children who may have difficulty completing the activity as described. Optional fine motor and educational extension activities suggest additional ways to target the skills addressed within the activity, plus ways to use the completed activity for art projects or to practice preacademic skills such as seriation and color and shape recognition.

Prerequisites of the Program

Before this program is implemented with any child, an occupational therapist should conduct a complete evaluation to determine that the child has the necessary prerequisite skills, to document the child's initial fine motor skills and to establish the appropriate placement within the program. It is not necessary for children to complete activities targeting skills they have already mastered. In addition, it is assumed that an occupational therapist will monitor children's progress and be available to advise nonprofessional or paraprofessional users when a child encounters difficulty.

It is suggested that the occupational therapist demonstrate the posture that children should maintain during these activities. In general, if the child is sitting, his or her feet should be flat on the floor and the hips and knees should be at a 90 degree angle. The surface should be an appropriate height so that the child's elbows and forearms can rest on it comfortably. Based on an evaluation of the child's skills, the occupational therapist may provide additional, individualized recommendations for positioning.

Among the other underlying motor skills that should be evaluated prior to a child's beginning the program are the following. Direct occupational therapy may be required prior to beginning this program if a child needs extra assistance with these prerequisite skills:

- adequate hand and body strength with balance and stability,
- midline crossing with emerging hand dominance,
- basic voluntary grasp and release patterns and
- bilateral hand use.

It is extremely important that the child also demonstrate cognitive and emotional readiness to engage in the types of activities within this program, including coloring, cutting and drawing. The occupational therapist should also determine each child's hand dominance and advise the adults implementing this program of the child's hand preference. Hand dominance should never be assumed without appropriate evaluation.

Because tactile defensiveness and sensory discriminatory difficulties are associated with poor in-hand manipulation skills, it is important for these conditions to be identified if present. It may be necessary to provide therapy in these areas either prior to or concomitant with initiating this program. Another factor deserving evaluation is motor planning ability. Because motor planning skills underlie the skills addressed in this program, it is not listed as a goal area. However, motor planning is a component of all the activities, so *Start to Finish* would benefit preschool children with motor planning difficulties by providing them with the extra practice and support they need to successfully learn and plan fine motor tasks. Participation in this program may not be sufficient therapy, however; and these children may benefit from additional direct occupational therapy.

Writing Names

An important component of the program is to begin teaching children to recognize and write their names. Children should attempt to write their names on every worksheet or paper project they complete. Here is a suggested sequence for teaching children to write their names. Begin by writing the child's name with a yellow marker and encouraging the child to trace over the letters with another marker to change the color of the name. Do not be concerned if the child has difficulty accurately tracing over the letters at first. Children who are unable to trace their names may draw scribbles, lines, circles and so forth, and identify these as their names. Children who are able to trace over their name with good accuracy should begin to imitate their names. Imitation means that they watch an adult write the name, then attempt to write it themselves. The next step is for children to copy their written names (i.e., they are given a written model of their names, but don't watch the adult write it out). It may be necessary to offer children greater assistance with selected portions of their names. For example, a child may be able to copy the first two letters in his or her name, but then need to trace the rest of the name. Some children will be able to write their names independently by the end of the program, but others will continue to need to copy or trace over their names. If you have concerns about whether a particular child's name-writing ability is age appropriate, please consult an occupational therapist.

Overview of Motor Development

This overview is primarily limited to the occupational therapy literature pertaining to fine motor skill development. It includes a summary of motor development and an in-depth discussion of specific fine motor skills that are targeted within the program; namely, in-hand manipulation, pencil grasp, scissors skills and grasp, and visual motor skills for handwriting and coloring. Finally, motor planning, which underlies all these skills, is addressed.

Typically, motor skills develop in a cephalo-caudal (i.e., head-to-toe) direction. This means that head control is typically achieved prior to walking (Klein, 1990b). At the same time, control of motor movements is achieved in a proximal-to-distal direction (i.e., trunk of the body to the limbs). Thus, controlled reach is typically achieved at the shoulder first, then at the elbow, wrist and fingers, in that order (Klein, 1990b). The proximal-to-distal development pattern implies that proximal stability (i.e., strength and control) at the trunk and shoulders must be established before distal fine motor control can be achieved. Although development occurs in this general chronological sequence, individual children often deviate somewhat from this pattern. Children often develop some fine motor skills before achieving complete proximal control. In addition, children accomplish whole-body movements before they learn to disassociate or separate movements (Klein, 1990a). For example, the first hand grasp children achieve involves using the entire hand in a flexion pattern, then gradually they disassociate the fingers and thumbs until they master refined grasps such as the pincer grasp (Klein, 1990b). Finally, the development of fine motor control can be influenced by numerous other areas, including cultural, social and cognitive factors; visual perceptual development; sensory integration; somatosensory function and vision (Exner, 1989, p. 235).

Development of In-Hand Manipulation Skills

In-hand manipulation is defined by Exner (1990, p. 64) as "the movement of an object within a person's hand, including adjustment of the object within the hand to allow for more effective placement for use or voluntary release." In-hand manipulation skills are important prerequisites to many activities of daily living as well as educational tasks. Children with delayed in-hand manipulation skills often appear clumsy and demonstrate delayed use and manipulation of writing utensils, scissors, clothing fasteners and small objects (Exner, 1992). Cornhill and Case-Smith (1996) identified in-hand manipulation as a significant contributing factor to precise and rapid manipulation of a writing tool for efficiency in handwriting. Humphry, Jewell and Rosenberger (1995) found a strong relationship between in-hand manipulation skills and coloring accuracy in a sample of typical children between two and seven years of age. Case-Smith (1995) found a significant relationship between in-hand manipulation skills and motor performance in preschool children with motor delays.

Numerous factors contribute to success at in-hand manipulation, including sensory information about the object, planning and sequencing of intrinsic hand movements, the child's hand size, and the meaning of the intended activity (Humphry, Jewell and Rosenberger, 1995). For example, Case-Smith (1991, p. 811) found that "children with both defensiveness and discrimination problems demonstrated the least efficiency on all of the in-hand manipulation tasks." This is why tactile defensiveness and sensory discrimination difficulties should be identified prior to initiating the *Start to Finish* curriculum.

Exner (1992) identified three broad categories of in-hand manipulation skills: *translation, rotation* and *shift.* Each of these types of skills can be used either in isolation or "while the individual is simultaneously stabilizing one or more other objects in the same hand" (Exner 1992, p. 40). Stabilization in conjunction with manipulation skills is more complex and difficult than in-hand manipulation alone.

Translation is the "linear movement of an object initially held in the palm to fingertips or the reverse movement of the object from fingertips to palm" (Jewell and Humphry, 1993, p. 69). An example of palm-to-finger translation is "moving a paper clip from the palm of the hand out to the fingertips for use on a piece of paper" (Exner, 1990, p. 65). Finger-to-palm translation is the opposite movement, such as one might do when moving a coin held between the thumb and fingers to the palm of the hand (Exner, 1992).

Rotation involves moving an object around one or more of its axes (Jewell and Humphry, 1993). Exner (1992, p. 40) defined *simple rotation* as "turning or rolling an object less than 180 degrees between the pads of the fingers and the pad of the thumb" (p. 40). Examples of simple rotation are rolling a ball of clay back and forth to form a snake and unscrewing a jar lid. *Complex rotation,* which involves rotating the object between 180 and 360 degrees, requires isolated, independent movements of the fingers, the thumb or both (Exner, 1992). Turning a paper clip so that the opposite end can be slid on a piece of paper and turning a pencil 180 degrees to use the eraser are examples of complex rotation (Jewell and Humphry, 1993).

Shift is defined as "the small linear movement of an object, often between the thumb and fingers" (Jewell and Humphry, 1993, p. 69). Activities that require shift include stringing beads (shifting the string and bead as the string goes through the bead), fanning several playing cards held in one hand and moving one's fingers down a pencil after it has been grasped in order to position them closer to the writing end (Exner, 1989, 1990).

Exner's (1995, p. 215) tentative developmental sequence of in-hand manipulation skill follows, with examples of each stage, derived from the sources cited below. According to Exner (1996), ongoing research suggests that finger-to-palm translation without stabilization (Stage 1) develops between approximately 12 and 15 months of age, and in-hand manipulation skills continue to be refined through at least 8 years of age (p. 278). More detailed information about the chronological ages at which specific skills are acquired cannot be given because the necessary normative data are not currently available. Remember, stabilization in conjunction with manipulation skills is more complex and difficult. In addition, it appears that in general children find it easiest to manipulate small objects. Tiny objects require precise finger control, whereas medium to large objects require control with more fingers, making both more difficult to manipulate than small objects (Exner 1996, p. 278).

Stage 1   Finger-to-palm translation: hiding a penny in one hand, crumpling paper (Exner, 1989, p. 251)

Stage 2   Palm-to-finger translation: moving a coin from the palm of the hand to the fingertips (Exner, 1992, p. 39)

Simple rotation: unscrewing jar lids (Exner 1992, p. 40)

Stage 3   Shift: buttoning, turning pages in a book (Exner, 1989, p. 252)

Complex rotation: turning a pencil within the hand in order to use the eraser (Exner, 1995, p. 216)

Development of a Mature Pencil Grasp

An efficient grip on writing implements is an important component of handwriting "because it allows the fine movements necessary for writing" (Schneck, 1991, p. 701). Benbow, Hanft and Marsh (1992, p. 23) identified the essential feature of an efficient grip as being that "the thumb and index finger form a circular web space allowing for skillful manipulation." Children follow a developmental progression through three general stages of pencil grasp: (a) palmar grasp, (b) static tripod grasp and (c) dynamic tripod grasp (Schneck and Henderson, 1990).

A *palmar grasp*—in which the writing instrument is positioned across the palm with the hand fisted and the wrist either supinated or pronated—is the most immature stage. In the second stage, *static tripod grasp,* the writing instrument is usually resting in the open web space opposed between the index pad and the thumb pad. In the *dynamic tripod grasp,* the writing instrument is held and controlled between the pads of the thumb and index finger and rests on the radial side of the middle finger (Rosenbloom and Horton, 1971). An important difference between the static and dynamic tripod pencil grasps is that in the static grasp the hand, fingers, wrist and pencil move as a single unit to control the writing instrument, whereas in the dynamic grasp, the fingers, hand and wrist are adjusted individually, giving more refined control of the writing instrument.

Schneck and Henderson (1990) further broke down these three stages into a developmental sequence of ten different grasps. Although an individual child does not generally demonstrate all ten of these grasps, it is useful to understand the range of grips that may be seen. Schneck and Henderson's operational definitions are as follows:

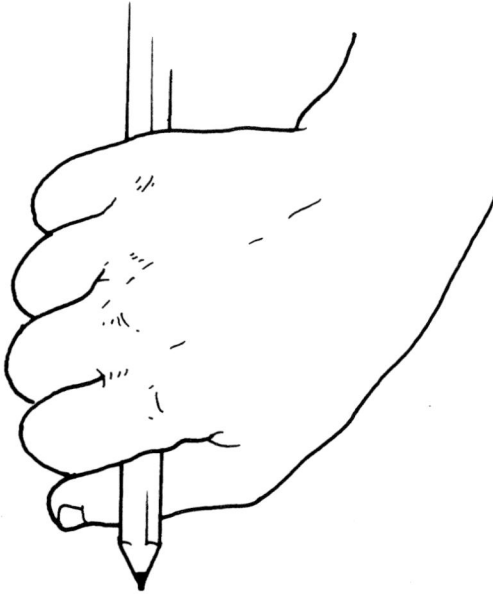

1. *Radial cross palmar grasp:* pencil positioned across palm projecting radially, held with fisted hand, forearm fully pronated, full arm movement (Morrison, 1978)

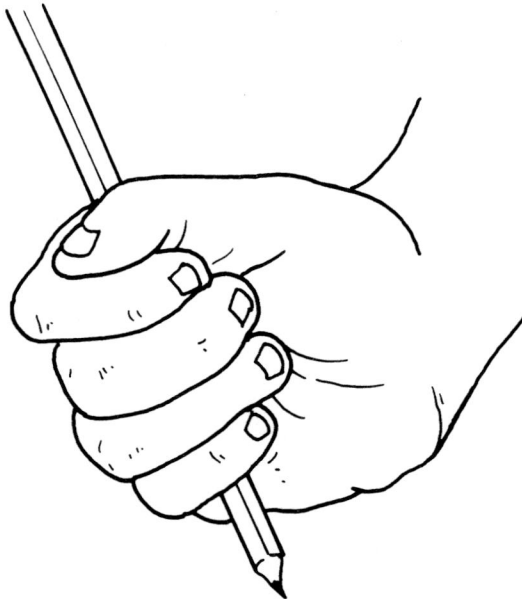

2. *Palmar supinate grasp:* pencil positioned across palm projecting ulnarly, held with fisted hand, wrist slightly flexed and supinated away from midpositon, full arm movement (Erhardt, 1984)

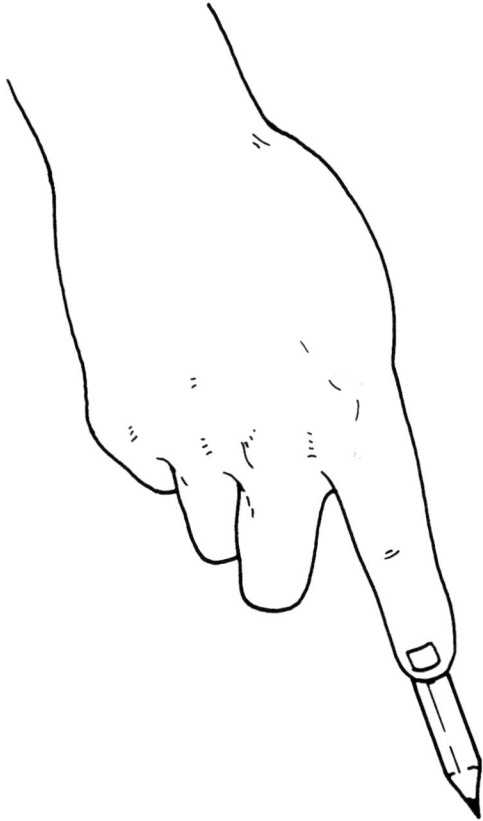

3. *Digital pronate grasp, only index finger extended:* pencil held in palmar grasp with index finger extended along pencil toward tip, arm not supported on table, full arm movement (Morrison, 1978)

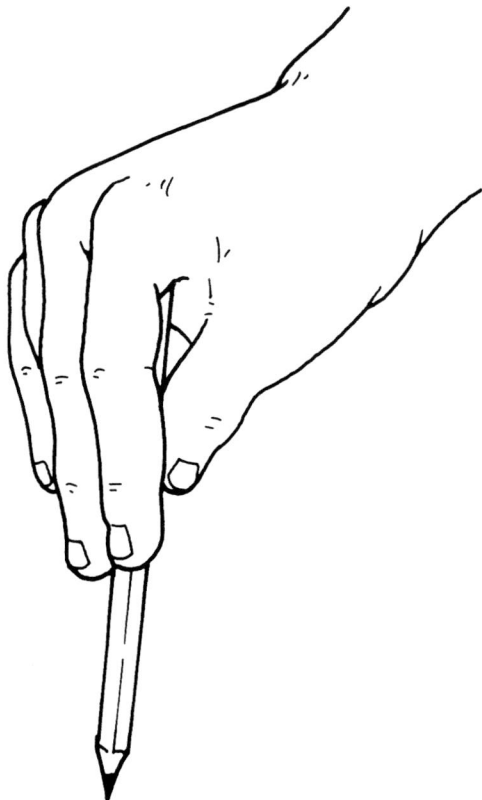

4. *Brush grasp:* pencil held with fingers with eraser end of pencil positioned against palm, hand pronated with wrist movement present, whole arm movement, forearm positioned in air

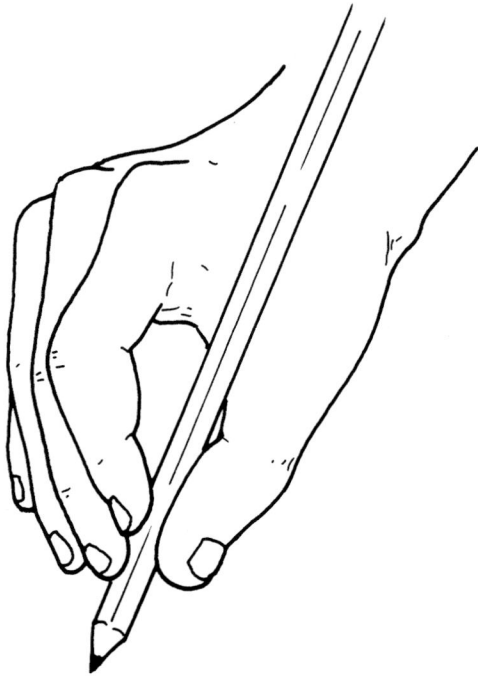

5. *Grasp with extended fingers:* pencil held with fingers, wrist straight and pronated with slight ulnar deviation, forearm moves as a unit

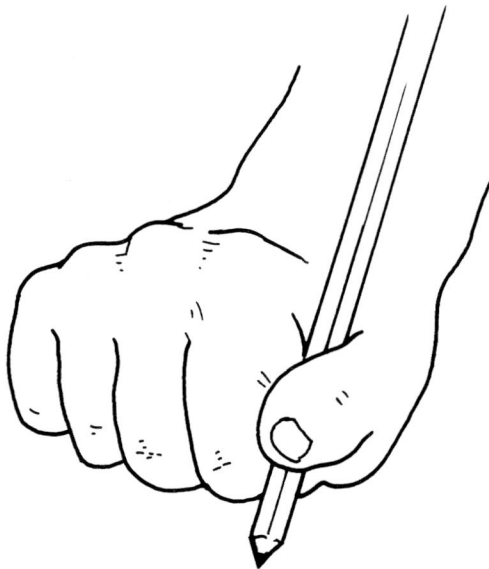

6. *Cross thumb grasp:* fingers fisted loosely into palm, pencil held against index finger with thumb crossed over pencil toward index finger, finger and wrist movement, forearm positioned on table (Gesell, 1940)

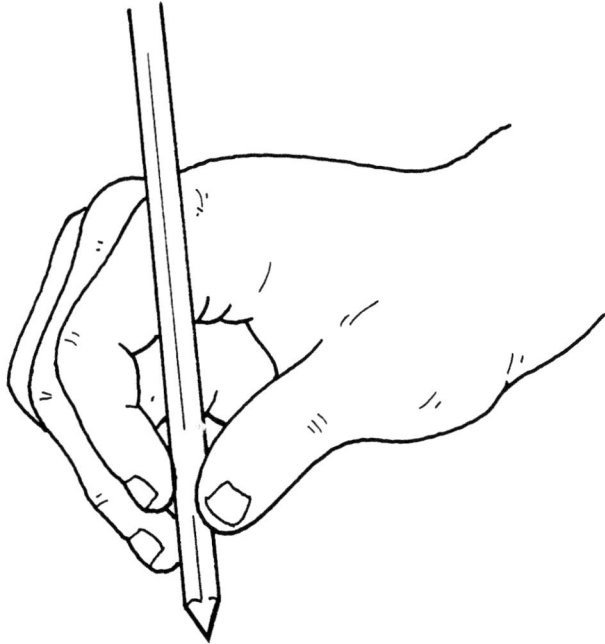

7. *Static tripod grasp:* pencil stabilized against radial side of third digit by thumb pulp with index pulp on top of shaft, thumb stabilized in full opposition, wrist slightly extended and hand moves as a unit, pencil rests in open web space, forearm resting on table (Rosenbloom and Horton, 1971)

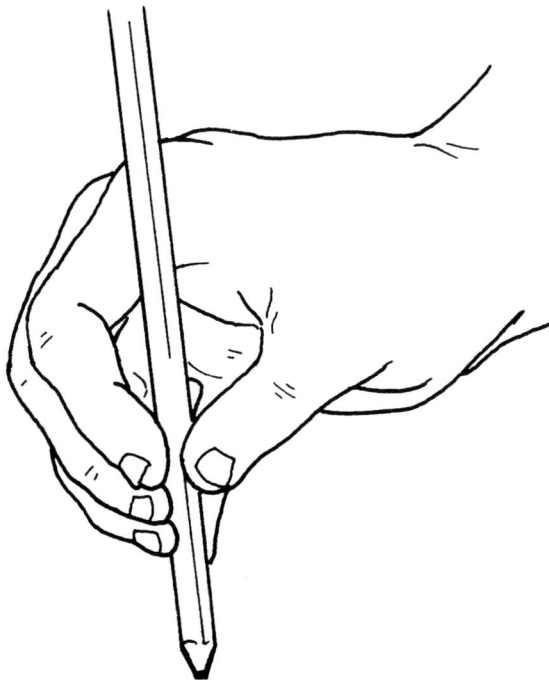

8. *Four finger grasp:* pencil held with four fingers in opposition, wrist and finger movement, forearm positioned on table

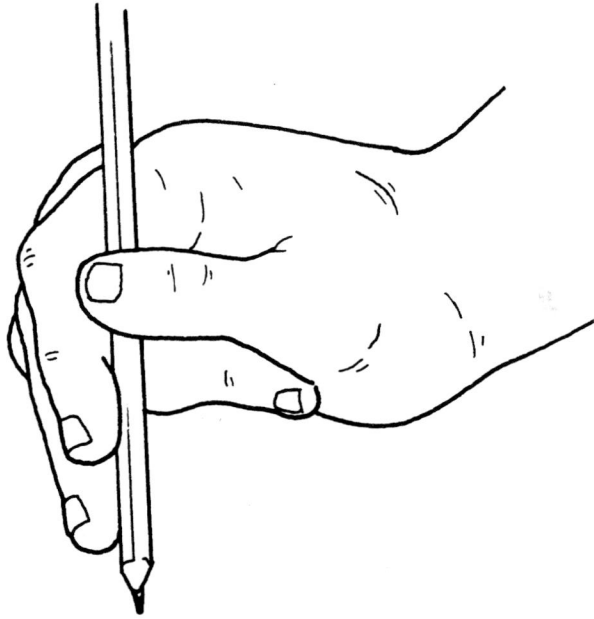

9. *Lateral tripod grasp:* pencil stabilized against radial side of third digit with index pulp on top of shaft of pencil, thumb adducted and braced over or under anywhere along the lateral border of index finger, wrist slightly extended, fourth and fifth digits flexed to stabilize metacarpophalangeal arch and third digit, localized movement of digits of tripod and wrist movements on tall and horizontal strokes, forearm resting on table (Schneck, 1987)

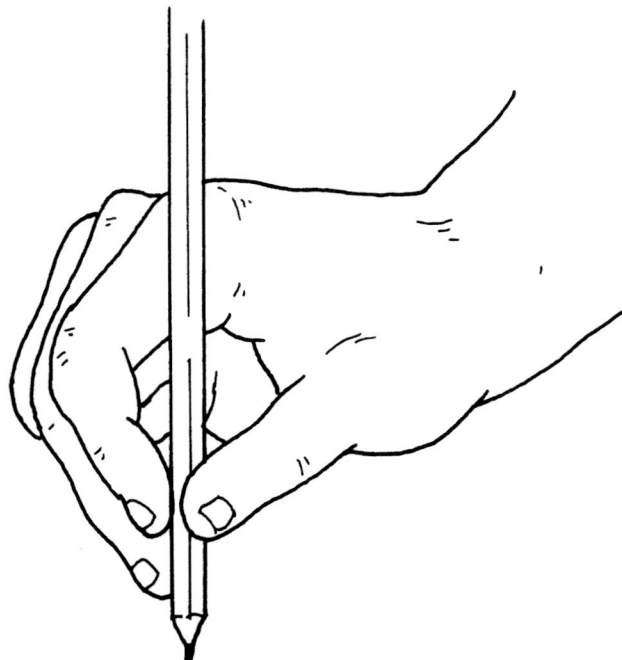

10. *Dynamic tripod grasp:* pencil stabilized against radial side of third digit by thumb pulp with index pulp on top of shaft of pencil, thumb stabilized in full opposition, wrist slightly extended, fourth and fifth digits flexed to stabilize the metacarpophalangeal arch and third digit, localized movement of digits of tripod and wrist movements on tall and horizontal strokes, forearm resting on table (Rosenbloom and Horton, 1971)

Note: (From Schneck and Henderson "Descriptive analysis of the developmental progression for pencil and crayon control in nondysfunctional children." Copyright 1990 by the American Occupational Therapy Association. Reprinted with permission.)

The dynamic and lateral tripod grasps are considered mature grips (Benbow, Hanft and Marsh, 1992; Schneck, 1991; Tseng and Cermak, 1993). Children generally achieve a mature pencil grasp between the ages of four and six years (Schneck, 1991; Schneck and Henderson, 1990; Tseng and Cermak, 1993). By second grade, a child's pencil grip is usually established and it is very difficult to modify after that time (Benbow, Hanft and Marsh, 1992). Remember that pencil grasp is used here to refer generically to grasping any writing implement.

Failure to develop a mature pencil grip may be caused by poor motor planning skills or impaired kinesthetic feedback (Tseng and Cermak, 1993). Motor planning difficulties cause inefficient pencil grips due to lack of accurate tactile and proprioceptive processing (Benbow, Hanft and Marsh, 1992). Figure 1 illustrates pencil grips that Benbow, Hanft and Marsh (1992) have identified as related to poor motor planning. Impaired kinesthetic, proprioceptive and tactile feedback may lead to an awkward grip, gripping the pencil with excessive pressure and intense visual monitoring of the precise movements of the pencil (Tseng and Cermak, 1993; Benbow, Hanft and Marsh, 1992). An extra tight grip leads to fatigue, shaking, wringing hands and stopping and starting frequently (Benbow, Hanft and Marsh, 1992).

Figure 1. Examples of inefficient pencil grips

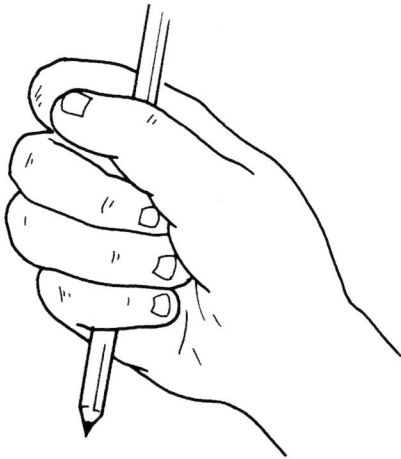

transpalmar

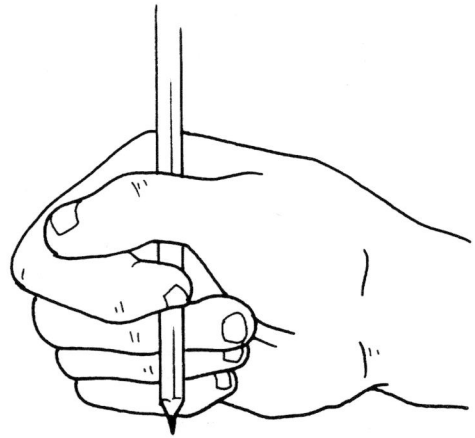

thumb wrap

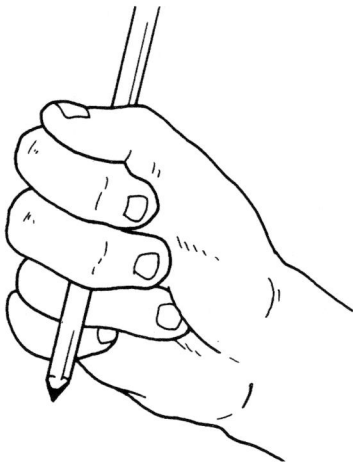

interdigital brace

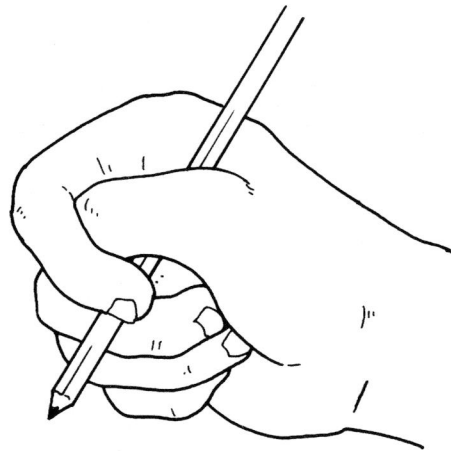

thumb tuck

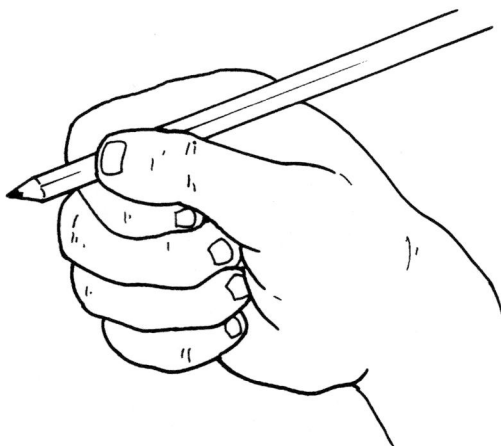

key or lateral pinch

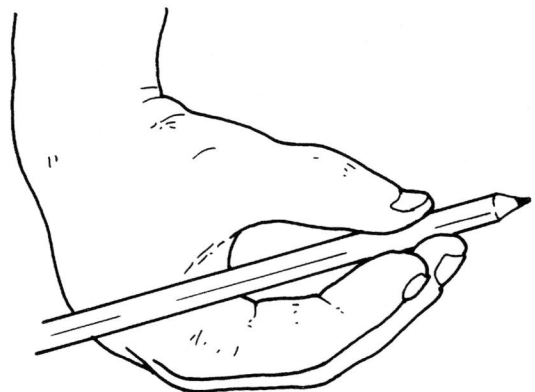

supinate

Development of a mature, functional pencil grasp is important because "inefficient grips limit the speed, range and fluidity of distal movements needed for writing" (Benbow, Hanft and Marsh, 1992, p. 24). In a study by Schneck (1991), first graders with mature pencil grasps demonstrated better writing skills than students with immature pencil grasps. While some variations in pencil grip may be functional for handwriting, efficient grips make handwriting easier (Tseng and Cermak 1993). The important areas to assess in order to determine whether a pencil grip is functional are stress points, fatigue, comfort and control (Benbow, Hanft and Marsh, 1992).

Visual, verbal and tactile cues may be helpful in assisting children to achieve an efficient pencil grip (Levine 1991). For example, Levine (1991, p. 319) suggested using tactile cues such as a rubber band or string wrapped around the writing implement, triangular pencil grippers and hexagonal-shaped crayons to assist a child in feeling and maintaining appropriate finger placement. A Stetro gripper adaptive device also works nicely to cue mature pencil grip. Writing on a vertical surface facilitates wrist extension, which also facilitates an efficient pencil grasp.

Development of Scissors Skills and Grasp

"Mastering the use of scissors is a necessary component of fine motor skill development in children, which occurs during the preschool years" (Schneck and Battaglia, 1992, p. 79). Scissors skills are needed for many school-related tasks, such as arts and crafts projects. Effective use of scissors requires proficiency in eye-hand coordination, motor planning, bilateral coordination, hand and finger dexterity and tool use. The child also must have reached the constructive stage of developmental play (Klein, 1990a). Klein (1990a, p. 23) described the following eleven-stage developmental sequence for scissors and precutting skills (the age ranges for skill acquisition are taken in part from *Development of Prewriting and Scissor Skills* [Levine, 1995] and the *Peabody Developmental Motor Scales* [Folio and Fewell, 1983]):

Skills acquired prior to age 3

> **Stage 1:** The child shows an interest in scissors
>
> **Stage 2:** The child holds and manipulates scissors appropriately
>
> **Stage 3:** The child opens and closes scissors in a controlled fashion
>
> **Stage 4:** The child cuts short random snips

Skills acquired between ages 3 and 5

> **Stage 5:** The child manipulates scissors in a forward motion
>
> **Stage 6:** The child coordinates the lateral direction of scissors
>
> **Stage 7:** The child cuts a straight forward line
>
> **Stage 8:** The child cuts simple geometric shapes

Skills acquired after age 5

> **Stage 9:** The child cuts simple figure shapes
>
> **Stage 10:** The child cuts complex figure shapes
>
> **Stage 11:** The child cuts nonpaper materials such as fabric and string

Various developmental progressions for cutting geometric shapes have been described by different authors; see Klein (1990a), Schneck and Battaglia (1992) and Stephens and Pratt (1989).

Schneck and Battaglia (1992, p. 81) give the following definition of a mature scissors grasp: "A mature scissors grip presupposes the ability to isolate thumb and fingers. The thumb of the preferred hand is inserted in one loop, while the middle, ring, or middle and ring fingers (depending on the size of the scissors' loops) are inserted in the other." The index finger is braced on the outside of the bottom loop for stability and strength and to direct the cutting activity (see figure 2). The piece of paper (or other material) being cut is held and manipulated by the nondominant hand, which is why cutting requires good bilateral coordination. A child who is just learning to cut may require assistance in holding and manipulating the paper and may hold the scissors with the wrist pronated (turned down) so the palm of the hand more or less faces the paper (see figures 3 and 4).

Figure 2. Mature scissors grasp

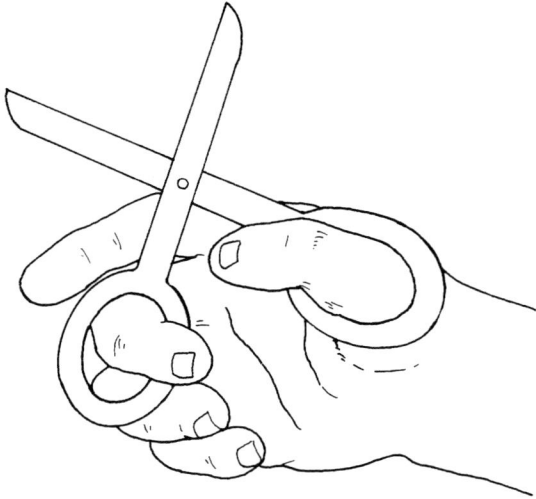

Figure 3. Holding scissors while manipulating paper

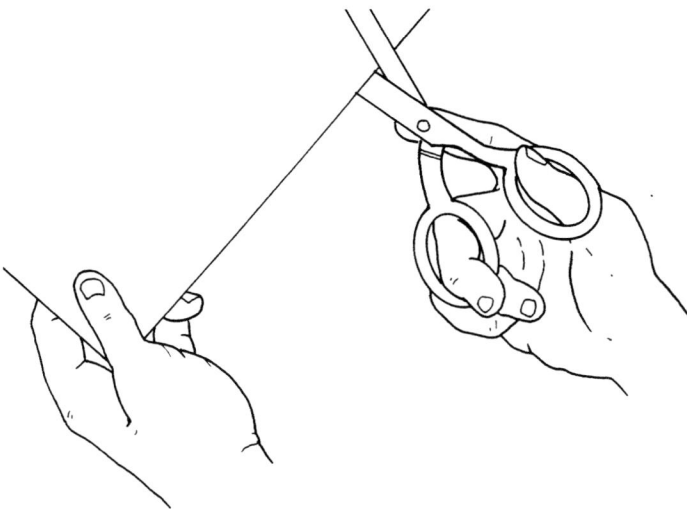

Figure 4. Immature scissors grasp with wrist pronated

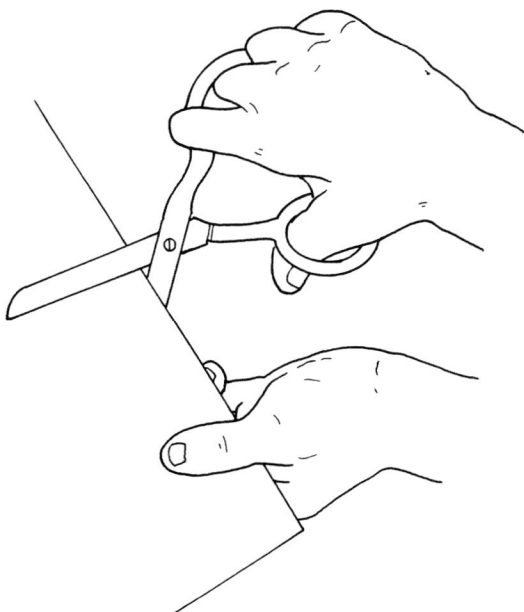

Initially, thick construction paper or some thick, hard materials such as modeling clay and straws are easier to cut. String and fabric are among the most difficult items to cut and should be introduced only after the child has mastered regular paper materials (Schneck and Battaglia, 1992). Klein (1987), as referenced in Schneck and Battaglia (1992), suggested the following progression of materials for cutting activities:

> index cards
> construction paper
> paper bags
> regular weight paper
> lightweight paper, such as wax paper or aluminum foil
> string or fabric

Development of Visual Motor Skills for Handwriting

Visual motor coordination—the ability to coordinate vision with the movements of the body (Stephens and Pratt, 1989)—is necessary for many functional and educational tasks. For example, drawing, copying forms and completing constructive tasks such as puzzles require good visual motor skills. Puzzles and other preschool manipulatives provide the visual motor basis for learning to write (Benbow, Hanft and Marsh, 1992), which is perhaps the most important visual motor task within the educational setting. Ziviani (1995) labeled the conceptual and perceptual motor abilities involved in drawing and writing *graphomotor skills.*

Cornhill and Case-Smith (1996, p. 734) identify the ability to integrate visual motor skills as an important variable in a child's handwriting ability. In order to copy, a child must visualize the letter form or shape, assign a meaning to the form and then manipulate a writing tool to reproduce the same letter form or shape. Numerous researchers have found a relationship between poor visual motor skills and poor handwriting. Weil and Cunningham-Amundson (1994) found a significant relationship between students' performance on the *Test of Visual Motor Integration* and their ability to copy letters legibly. Tseng and Murray (1994) found that poor handwriters scored worse than good handwriters on most of the perceptual motor tests they administered.

In a study of kindergarten students, Weil and Cunningham-Amundson (1994) advised that handwriting instruction not be initiated until a child is able to copy the following shapes: vertical line, horizontal line, circle, cross, right oblique line, square, left oblique line, oblique cross and triangle. Klein (1990b, p. 22) provided the following development sequence of visual motor skills for handwriting (the age ranges for skill acquisition are taken in part from the *Peabody Developmental Motor Scales* [Folio and Fewell, 1983] and the *Developmental Test of Visual-Motor Integration* [Beery and Buktenica, 1989]).

Skills acquired prior to age 2

Stage 1: The child mouths crayons or crinkles paper

Stage 2: The child bangs crayons on paper

Stage 3: The child scribbles randomly

Stage 4: The child scribbles spontaneously in a horizontal direction

The child scribbles spontaneously in a vertical direction

Stage 5: The child scribbles spontaneously in a circular direction

Stage 6: The child imitates a horizontal scribble direction

The child imitates a vertical scribble direction

The child imitates a circular scribble direction

Skills acquired between ages 2 and 3

Stage 7: The child imitates a horizontal line

The child imitates a vertical line

The child imitates a circular line

Stage 8: The child copies a horizontal line

The child copies a vertical line

Skills acquired between ages 3 and 5

Stage 9: The child copies a circle

The child imitates a cross (+)

Stage 10: The child copies a cross (+)

The child imitates a right-to-left diagonal (/)

Stage 11: The child copies a right-to-left diagonal (/)

The child imitates a square

Stage 12: The child copies a square

The child imitates a left-to-right diagonal (\)

Stage 13: The child copies a left-to-right diagonal (\)

The child imitates an X

Stage 14: The child copies an X

The child imitates a triangle

Skills acquired after age 5

Stage 15: The child copies a triangle

The child imitates a diamond

Stage 16: The child copies a diamond

Different stages of learning to write have been described. Benbow, Hanft and Marsh (1992) described a two-step process of writing production. The first involves tracing letter forms, in which the eyes direct the hand to follow visual cues of curves or angles. The second step is imitation: the student watches an action (e.g., the teacher drawing a shape), then draws the same shape, glancing alternately between the visual model (i.e.; the teacher's shape) and his or her own production. Cunningham-Amundson (1992) suggested a sequence for teaching children to copy handwriting within the academic setting. The steps children would typically master during preschool and kindergarten are these:

1. The teacher verbally and physically models the action to be performed.

2. The child traces the shape or letter.

3. The verbal and physical cues are gradually faded.

4. The student copies the shape or letter, which involves observing the end product and attempting to reproduce it without seeing a model of the item being drawn.

5. The teacher dictates letters or shapes for the child to write or draw.

The complete sequence may not be necessary for all children: children with perceptual motor deficits may require both tracing and fading of cues as steps in reaching the copying stage, whereas other children may require only a model in order to imitate a letter correctly (Cunningham-Amundson, 1992, p. 71). A child would typically reach the fourth or fifth stage by the end of kindergarten (age 5 or 6). Later stages are not detailed here because they are not relevant to the program. In brief, the child develops proficiency in combining letters and words, in self-correcting mistakes and in correcting mistakes based on peer feedback.

Development of Visual Motor Skills for Coloring

Visual motor coordination is a necessary component for stroke control and accuracy in learning to color, a skill required frequently in the primary grades. Coloring is also a precursor skill for the development of other, more advanced fine motor skills.

Klein (1990b) provided a developmental sequence for stroke control and the ability to color within a picture area. Initially, a child covers a large piece of paper with random lines, often coloring off the paper. Then, the child learns to grossly cover an 8½" x 11" sheet of paper with random color. Next, the child colors a medium-sized geometric area using a consistent stroke direction. Then the child colors a small geometric shape, adjusting the paper to the stroke. Color choice begins to become a factor. Next, the child learns to color medium-sized designs, adjusting the paper to accommodate the stroke direction and control. Finally, the child will color a small design with accurate attention to detail and color choice, holding the paper still and adjusting the stroke to fit the area. According to the *Peabody Developmental Motor Scales* (Folio and Fewell, 1983), by approximately 60 months of age children should be able to color between two lines 1/2 inch apart without crossing the lines more than twice, and with color filling 3/4 of the space.

Motor Planning for Fine Motor Skills

Motor planning refers to the ability to carry out skilled, nonhabitual motor acts in the correct sequence, which is a very necessary component of all fine motor skills (Benbow, Hanft and Marsh, 1992). Examples of motor planning tasks within an educational setting are copying a shape or letter and sequencing cutting. Motor planning requires the ability to retrieve a consistent motor pattern. Children who have difficulty retrieving a motor pattern may rely heavily on vision to monitor their completion of fine motor tasks. Because children with motor planning difficulties need more assistance and cues to learn and sequence tasks, they require more practice when learning fine motor skills. They may also require other adaptations such as verbal cues to sequence and plan the task, a longer time for completion, and assistance in organizing and spacing the task (Benbow, Hanft and Marsh, 1992). Finally, as noted previously, it is not unusual for such children to demonstrate inefficient pencil grips. Motor planning skills underlie all the skills addressed in this program.

Summary of Motor Development

According to Case-Smith (1995, p. 31), "the preschool years seem to be a critical period for the development of hand skills." Between three and five years of age, children demonstrate rapid gains in fine motor skills such as manipulation, eye-hand coordination and tool use. The fine motor skills targeted within this preschool program should assist in the refinement of hand skills for school-readiness activities such as handwriting, cutting and coloring. The graphic in figure 5 demonstrates how the various fine motor skills targeted in the program underlie handwriting, coloring and cutting ability. Beginning at the base of the pyramid, each skill listed is prerequisite to the one above it. Thus, motor planning underlies visual motor control and in-hand manipulation, which in turn underlie pencil and scissor grasps and all precoloring, prewriting and precutting skills. The two-way arrows indicate that these skills develop simultaneously, with development in one skill influencing development in the other.

Figure 5. Developmental Relationships among Fine Motor Skills

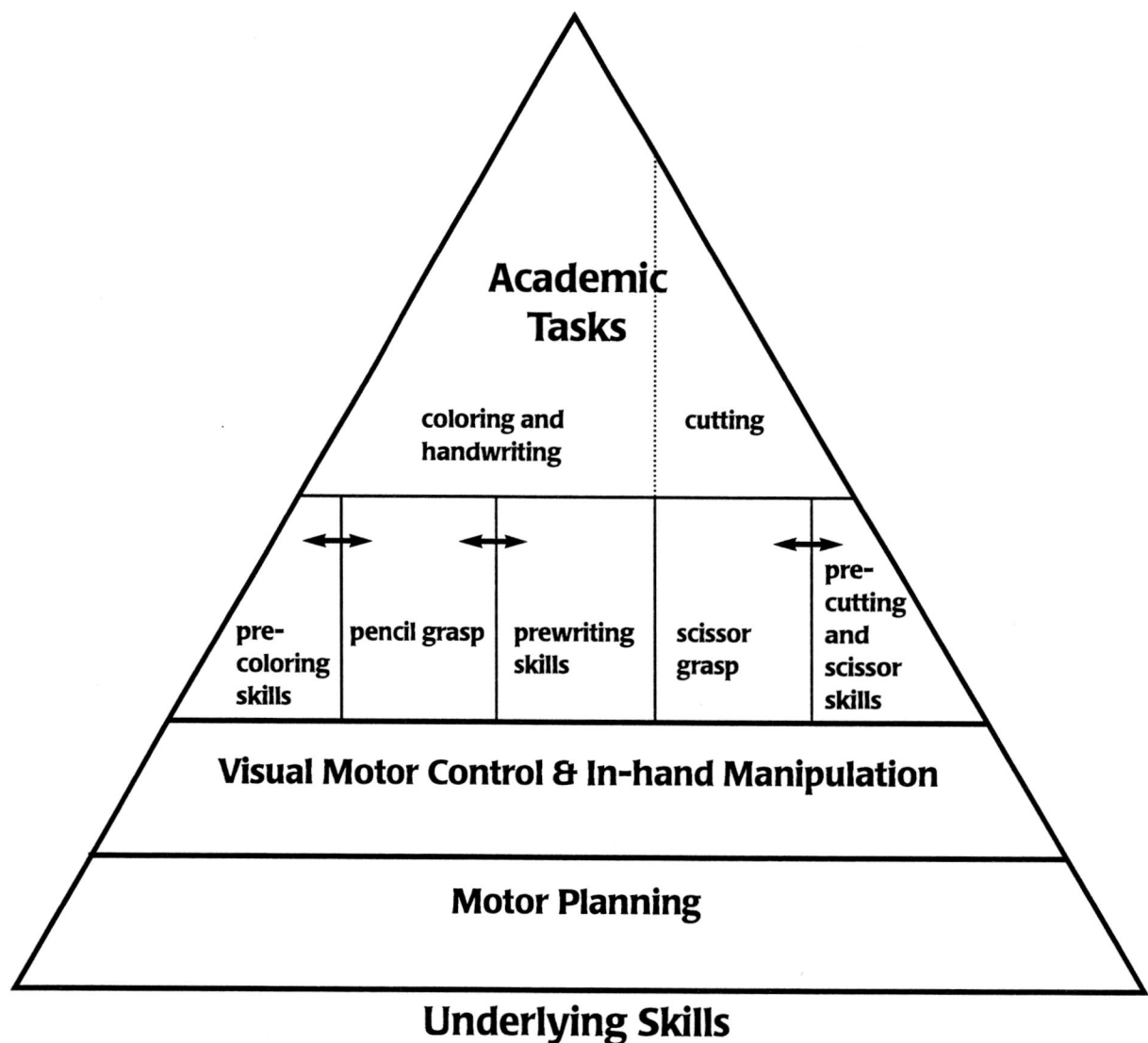

In-hand manipulation skills are important not only for manipulating writing utensils or scissors, but also for such daily living skills as buttoning a jacket and opening a milk carton. Developing a mature pencil grasp—i.e., a dynamic tripod grasp or lateral tripod grasp—is important for achieving efficiency, dexterity and comfort with handwriting. An immature pencil grasp may cause fatigue and decrease the amount of control for writing. Developing a mature scissors grasp and cutting skills requires proficiency in eye-hand coordination, motor planning, bilateral coordination, hand and finger dexterity and tool use. Cutting is needed in art or craft projects as well as daily life activities.

Good visual motor skills have been associated with success in handwriting, drawing pictures and coloring. Motor planning difficulties may delay the development of fine motor coordination. Children with motor planning difficulties may require more cues for sequencing and extra practice to develop the fine motor skills targeted within the preschool classroom.

The
Start to Finish
Program

Unit 1

Activity 1: Stringing Medium-Sized Beads

Skill areas addressed
✔ in-hand manipulation, visual motor skills

Goal
✔ The child will independently string beads without any cues.

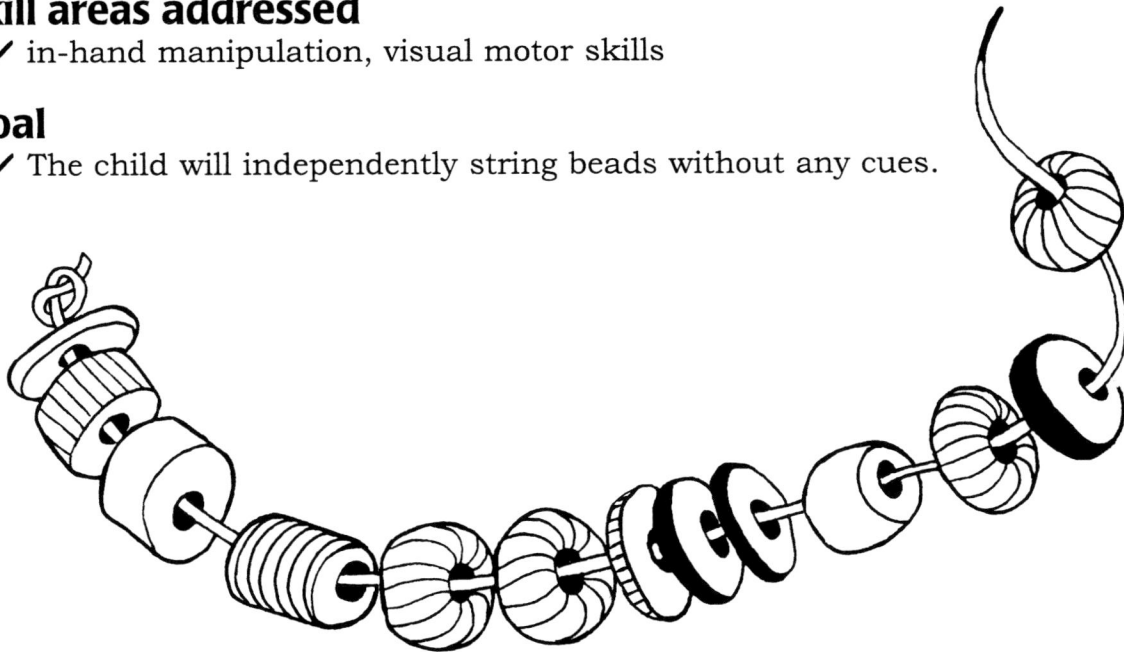

Supplies Needed

12-15 medium beads (1" to $1\frac{1}{2}$" in diameter) with a hole at least $\frac{1}{4}$" in diameter

1 string with a hard tip, at least 12" long (A thin shoelace works well.)

Instructions

Knot the end of the string so the beads will not slip off. Place all the loose beads and the string in front of the child. Instruct the child to string all the beads. Then encourage the child to remove the beads and string them again.

Suggested Modifications and Adaptations

- Provide a demonstration of stringing the beads.
- If the child has difficulty, provide verbal cues and hand-over-hand assistance as necessary until the child is successful.
- If the child continues to have difficulty, hold the string at the end of the hard tip. Have the child place the bead on the tip, then demonstrate how to thread the bead onto the string.
- To make the activity even easier, provide large flattish beads that have large holes (at least $\frac{1}{2}$" in diameter), and in which the width of the bead that the string goes through is less than $\frac{1}{2}$".
- Consult the OT if the child continues to have difficulty despite modifications.

Activity 1: Stringing Medium-Sized Beads (cont.)

Optional Fine Motor or Educational Extension Activities

- Have the child string beads to make a necklace for dress-up.
- Use the beads for counting activities; for example, by having the child count the number of loose beads, then the number of beads on the string, then add or remove beads and count again.
- Complete sequencing and patterning activities with the beads.
- Make a necklace of cereal loops, using cereals such as Cheerios or Froot Loops.

Activity 6: Snipping Narrow Paper Strips

Skill areas addressed

✔ in-hand manipulation, visual motor skills, scissors skills and grasp

Goal

✔ The child will independently make at least 10 cuts all the way through a strip of tagboard $1/2$" wide.

Supplies Needed

Child safety scissors

Strips of thin cardboard or tagboard (at least 5" in length and no more than $1/2$" wide).

Instructions

Instruct the child to make a series of cuts through the width of the tagboard strip (cutting all the way through the strip). Encourage the child to snip each strip many times. When first learning to hold scissors, some children turn down (pronate) the wrist so that the palm faces toward the paper rather than being at a 90° angle to it. Encourage the child to use a "thumb-up" position, but if this is difficult, the pronated position is acceptable at this level.

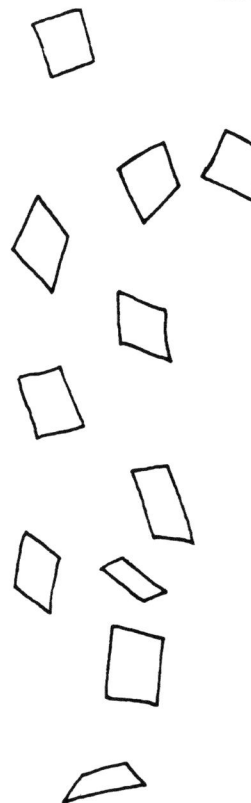

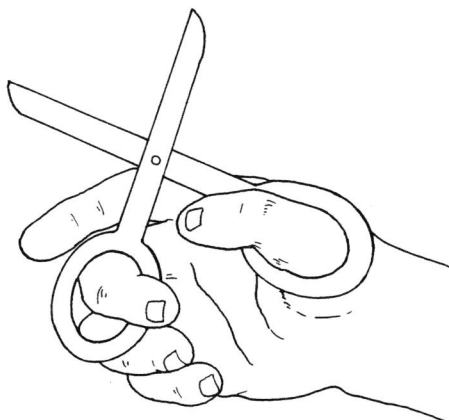

Correct, "thumb up" grasp

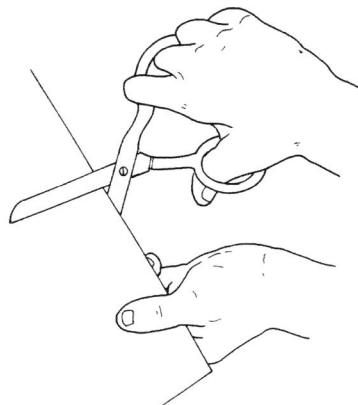

Immature, pronated grasp

Activity 6: Snipping Narrow Paper Strips (cont.)

Suggested Modifications and Adaptations

- Demonstrate the activity.
- If the child has difficulty holding the paper and manipulating the scissors at the same time, hold the paper for the child.
- If the child is having difficulty, provide hand-over-hand assistance, then fade to verbal cues alone as the child gains independence.
- Assist the child to achieve a correct scissors grasp and orientation to paper as necessary.

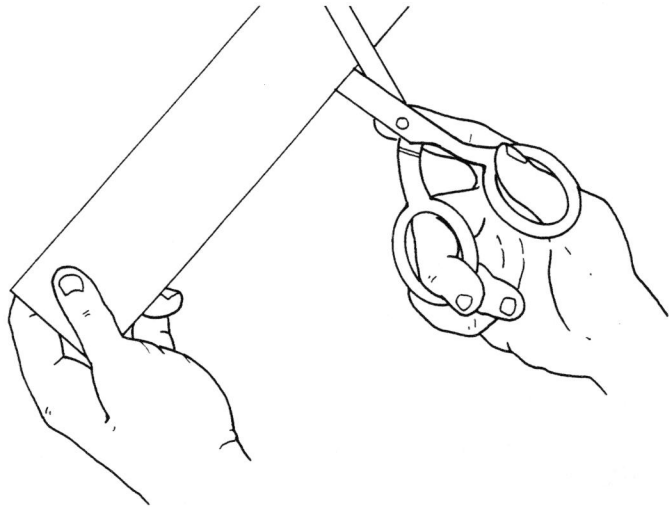

Holding scissors while manipulating paper

- If the child has significant difficulty using regular preschool safety scissors, consult the OT to determine whether adapted scissors might be appropriate.

Optional Fine Motor or Educational Extension Activities

- Vary the types of materials the child snips. The material should be thicker than construction paper, easy to cut through and approximately 1/2" in width. Possible materials include modeling clay, straws or laminated strips of paper. (Do not use fabric or yarn.)
- Place sheets and strips of paper of various sizes in a large tub. Then encourage the child to cut and snip the sheets of paper however he or she chooses.
- After snipping numerous strips of paper, the child may glue the pieces onto a large sheet of construction paper to make a picture.
- Count the number of snips in each strip of paper or classify the strips according to color or length.

Activity 8: Teddy Bear Lace-Up

Skill areas addressed

✔ in-hand manipulation, visual motor skills

Goal

✔ The child will independently thread a lace through at least 8 holes (not necessarily adjacent holes), pulling the string tight.

Supplies Needed

A laminated photocopy of the "Teddy Bear Lace-up" worksheet (or cover with clear plastic shelf paper)

Hole punch

A thin shoelace or piece of yarn at least 20" long (Wrap the end in tape or dip it into glue to make a hard tip for ease of threading through the holes.)

Instructions

In advance: Cut out the bear outline. Punch out all the marked holes around the edge. Knot or loop the end of the shoelace or yarn so the child can pull it tight against the first hole (put a small bead on the end, if necessary).

With the child: Instruct the child to lace in and out of all the holes, pulling the string tight each time. Encourage the child to thread the lace through all the holes. (However, it is not necessary to lace all the holes in sequential order; the child can skip around among the holes.) Encourage the child to take the string out and lace the bear repeatedly until he or she becomes proficient with the activity.

Suggested Modifications and Adaptations

- Demonstrate how to pull the lace through a hole until it is tight.
- If the child is having difficulty, provide hand-over-hand assistance, fading to verbal cues alone as the child gains independence.
- Increase the size of the holes to $3/4$" diameter so that the string is easier to pull through.

Activity 8: Teddy Bear Lace-Up (cont.)

- If the number of holes appears to confuse the child, punch out only the holes across the bottom of the bear. Have the child lace these. Gradually increase the number of holes as the child gains confidence.

Optional Fine Motor or Educational Extension Activities

- Allow the child to practice with other commercially manufactured lacing boards.
- Have the child practice lacing up shoes.
- This suggestion works best if several children are doing the lacing activity. Allow each child to color a bear before it is laminated, then choose a color of yarn to lace it with. However, it is not expected that the child color with accuracy at this point in the program. Encourage the children to use their bears as puppets in dramatic play or storytelling activities. Allow them to take their bears home at the end of the week.
- Read children's stories about bears, such as *Winnie the Pooh* or the Paddington Bear or Berenstain Bears series. The child may use the lace-up bear to act out parts of the story, if desired.

Teddy Bear Lace-Up

Activity 9: It's a Snap

Skill areas addressed

✔ in-hand manipulation, visual motor skills

Goal

✔ The child will independently snap 4 snaps.

Supplies Needed

A commercially manufactured or homemade snap board or vest with at least 4 snaps (Any clothing item that has at least 4 snaps will also work. However, make sure the snaps are not too difficult to push together.)

Instructions

Demonstrate how to push the snaps together. Instruct the child to snap at least 4 snaps. Then have the child unsnap all the snaps. Encourage the child to continue practicing until he or she becomes proficient.

Suggested Modifications and Adaptations

- Provided repeated demonstrations and models of the actions required for snapping.
- If the child is having difficulty, provide hand-over-hand assistance, then fade to verbal cues alone as the child gains independence.

Optional Fine Motor or Educational Extension Activities

- Vary the size and types of snaps used.
- To make the activity more difficult, have the child put on a jacket, vest or shirt with snaps, then practice snapping and unsnapping the garment.
- Provide garments that have snaps and other fasteners for children to use when playing dress-up or house.

Activity 11: Big-Button Button-Up

Skill areas addressed

✔ in-hand manipulation, visual motor skills

Goal

✔ The child will independently button and unbutton 3 large buttons.

Supplies Needed

Buttoning board or vest with 3 or more buttons $3/4$" to $1\,1/4$" in diameter. (A shirt or jacket with at least 3 buttons of the designated size may also be used. Or you can make a homemade buttoning board by sewing buttons and button-holes on a piece of fabric.)

Instructions

Demonstrate how to push the buttons through the buttonholes. Then instruct the child to button all the buttons and unbutton them again (the child should do at least 3 buttons). Encourage the child to continue practicing until he or she becomes proficient with buttoning and unbuttoning.

Suggested Modifications and Adaptations

- Provide repeated demonstrations and models of the actions required for buttoning and unbuttoning.
- If the child is having difficulty, provide hand-over-hand assistance with pulling the buttons through the holes. Fade to verbal cues alone as the child gains independence.
- If the child continues to have difficulty, place the buttons partway through the holes, then have the child pull them the rest of the way through.
- If the child is becoming frustrated because the activity is too difficult, increase the size of the buttonholes to more than twice the size of the buttons. Have the child practice pulling the buttons through those holes. When the child is proficient with these buttonholes, try the original activity again. (If this is too big a jump, you can gradually decrease the size of the holes by putting a few stitches in the large buttonholes each time the child repeats the activity.)

Activity 11: Big-Button Button-Up (cont.)

Optional Fine Motor or Educational Extension Activities

- Vary the size and type of buttons used.
- To make the activity more difficult, have the child put on a jacket, vest or shirt, then practice buttoning and unbuttoning the garment while wearing it.
- Provide a large container of loose buttons. Classify and seriate the buttons by size, color, shape, etc.
- Provide clothes with large buttons for the children to use when playing dress-up or house.

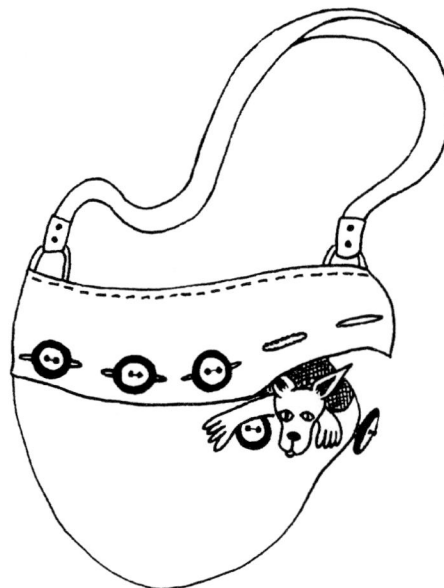

Activity 12: Imitating Circles

Skill areas addressed

✔ in-hand manipulation, visual motor skills, prewriting skills, pencil grasp

Goal

✔ The child will independently imitate at least 10 circles.

Supplies Needed

Washable, nontoxic markers (medium sized)

Paper

Vertical board: either tape butcher paper to a wall at the child's level or use an easel

Circular scribbles

Instructions

First have the child watch you make several separate circles on the vertical surface with markers. Then instruct the child to imitate exactly what you have done. Have the child make at least 10 circles. Encourage the child to attempt to make a circle rather than just circular scribbles (i.e., the beginning and ending points meet or nearly meet).

Suggested Modifications and Adaptations

• Demonstrate the activity.
• Hand-over-hand physical assistance may be necessary at first to help the child feel the motion of making circles. Then fade to verbal cues only.

Circles

Activity 12: Imitating Circles (cont.)

- Provide verbal cues if the child is having difficulty stopping the circle where it began (instead of continuing to go around and around in circular scribbles). Sometimes it is helpful to say "circle" when the child begins the motion and to say "stop" when the child circles around once. Encourage the child to say these cues as well.

Optional Fine Motor or Educational Extension Activities

- Repeat the activity with a variety of media:
  With paints on paper, standing at an easel
  With markers or crayons on paper, sitting at a table
  With chalk, standing at a chalkboard
  With shaving cream or talcum powder on the tabletop, or with finger-paints on paper (sitting)
  With a drawing toy such as a Magna Doodle (sitting)
- Have the child make circles with different colors of markers, then categorize the circles by color and size.
- Have the child identify as many things as possible in the room that are circular in shape.

Activity 13: Hole Punch Art

Skill areas addressed

✔ visual motor skills, in-hand manipulation, scissors skills and grasp

Goal

✔ The child will independently punch 10 holes by pushing the handles of the hole punch together with one hand while holding the paper to be punched in the other hand.

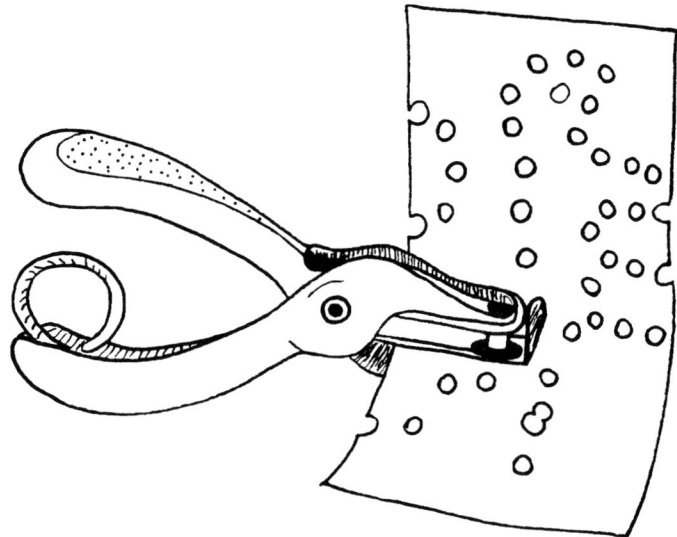

Supplies Needed

Construction paper

Hand-held hole punch (Do not use one of the hole punches that can be placed on a table and pushed down with the palm of one hand.)

Instructions

First demonstrate how to punch holes, with emphasis on placing the paper in the hole punch and pushing the handles together. Then ask the child to punch holes in the paper. Encourage the child to continue punching holes until he or she uses the hole punch proficiently. The child can choose to punch random holes or to punch out designs in the paper.

Suggested Modifications and Adaptations

• Provide repeated demonstrations and models of the required actions.
• If the child is having difficulty, provide hand-over-hand assistance, then fade to verbal cues as the child gains independence.

Activity 13: Hole Punch Art (cont.)

Optional Fine Motor or Educational Extension Activities

- Punch out a simple design, such as a geometric shape. Encourage the child to imitate the design. Label the different shapes you make.
- Copy a large picture of a simple object (such as a ball, an animal, an apple) and mark X's at regular intervals around the edge of the object. (It may be helpful to laminate the picture or cover it with clear plastic shelf paper.) Have the child punch holes at the X's, then use the picture for a lacing activity.
- With a similar large picture of a single object, have the child punch overlapping holes around the silhouette of the object to "cut" it out.

Activity 14: Fold-over Fun

Skill areas addressed

✔ visual motor skills, in-hand manipulation

Goal

✔ The child will make a crease in a sheet of paper to fold it.

Supplies Needed

Thick construction paper

Adult scissors

Washable, nontoxic markers or crayons

Instructions

First demonstrate how to fold the paper in half, emphasizing matching up the edges of the paper and pushing down on the fold with one finger to crease it. Then instruct the child to fold a sheet of paper in half. (At this stage, emphasize making a crease in the paper; it is not critical that the child exactly match up the edges of the paper.) Encourage the child to continue folding the sheet of paper, or to fold other sheets of paper, until he or she can fold easily. Then take a sheet of paper that has been folded once. Allow the child to color the paper however he or she wishes. Stand the folded paper up easel-style to display the picture. If necessary, you can trim the bottom edges of the paper so the fold-over will stand straight.

Suggested Modifications and Adaptations

- Provide repeated models and demonstrations of the action of folding.
- If the child is having difficulty, provide hand-over-hand assistance, emphasizing pushing down on the fold to crease the paper. Then phase to verbal cues alone as the child gains independence.

Activity 14: Fold-over Fun (cont.)

Optional Fine Motor or Educational Extension Activities

- Vary the type of paper used and the size of the sheet.
- Provide a fresh piece of paper and encourage the child to fold it many times. Then unfold the sheet and count together how many creases are in it.
- Make a fold-over farm or zoo: Encourage the child to make several fold-overs and draw an animal on each one with crayons. Cut out the animals for the child. Allow the child to engage in fantasy play with the animals.

Activity 15: Getting Down to Nuts & Bolts

Skill areas addressed

✔ in-hand manipulation, visual motor skills

Goal

✔ The child will independently screw together and unscrew at least 5 nuts and bolts.

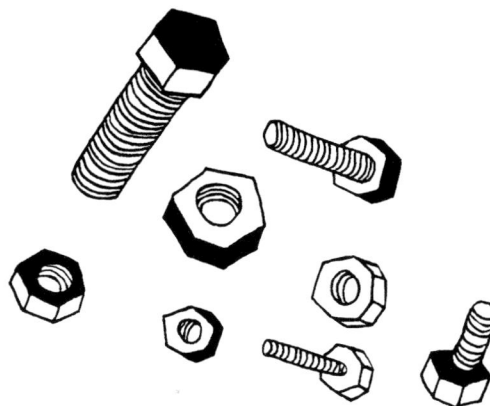

Supplies Needed

8-12 nuts and matching bolts in various sizes between $3/8$" and $3/4$" in diameter (Make sure that each bolt fits only one of the nuts.)

Instructions

Demonstrate how to screw the nuts onto the bolts. Then separate the nuts into one pile and the bolts into another. Instruct the child to match up and screw together the nuts and bolts. Then let the child take them all apart again.

Suggested Modifications and Adaptations

- Provide additional models or demonstrations of the activity.
- If the child is having difficulty, provide hand-over-hand assistance. Fade to verbal cues as the child gains independence.
- If the child has difficulty with real nuts and bolts because of their small size, offer large toy plastic nuts and bolts (such as those made by Fisher Price). When the child becomes proficient with the toys, progress to regular nuts and bolts.

Optional Fine Motor or Educational Extension Activities

- To make the activity more difficult, include some bolts that are smaller than $3/8$" in diameter.
- Use commercial nuts-and-bolts boards. (You can make a homemade version by screwing several bolts through a piece of plywood, spaced several inches apart.)
- Classify and seriate the bolts and nuts based on size.
- Look for furniture and other items in the room that are built with nuts and bolts. Talk about the many different kinds of things that nuts and bolts can be used to build. What kinds of workers might use nuts and bolts?

Activity 16: Snipping Wider Strips

Skill areas addressed

✔ in-hand manipulation, visual motor skills, scissors skills and grasp

Goal

✔ The child will independently cut across a strip of paper 1" wide at least 10 times.

Supplies Needed

Child safety scissors

8-12 (or more) strips of construction paper, no more than 1" wide and at least 5" in length

Instructions

Instruct the child to make a series of snips all the way across the width of a strip of paper. (Assist the child to place the fingers in the scissor loops correctly.) Encourage the child to use a "thumb-up" position, but if this is too difficult, the pronated wrist position, with the palm facing more or less down is acceptable at this level. Prompt the child to snip across each strip of paper many times.

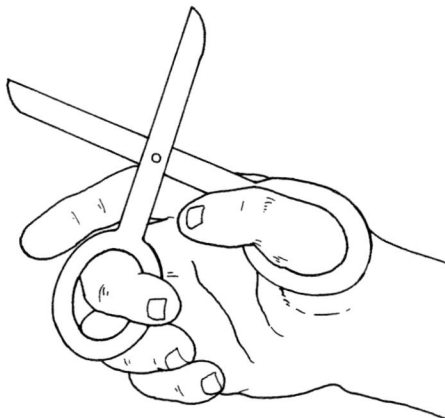

Correct, "thumb up" grasp

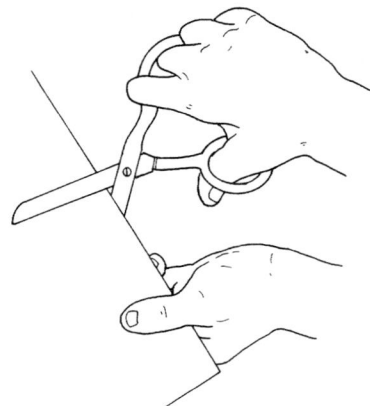

Immature, pronated grasp

Activity 16: Snipping Wider Strips (cont.)

Suggested Modifications and Adaptations

- Demonstrate the activity.
- If the child has difficulty holding the paper and manipulating the scissors at the same time, hold the paper for the child.
- Use tagboard instead of construction paper strips to give the child an easier material to cut.
- If the child is having difficulty cutting with the scissors, provide hand-over-hand assistance, then fade to verbal cues alone as the child gains independence.

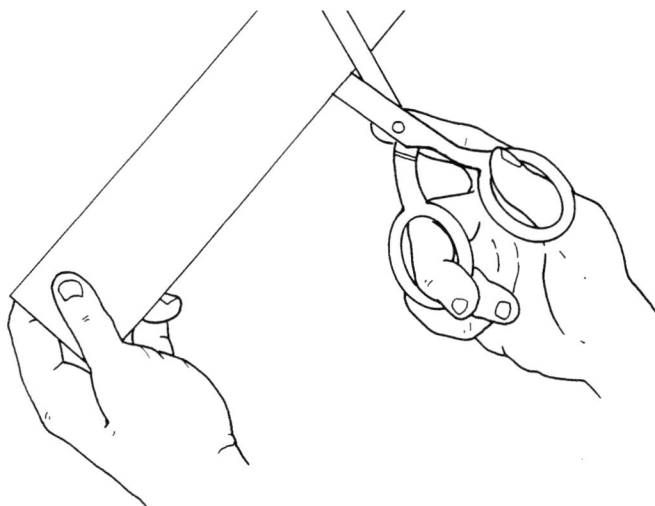

Holding scissors while manipulating paper

- Assist the child to achieve a correct scissors grasp and orientation to paper as necessary.

Optional Fine Motor or Educational Extension Activities

- Vary the types of materials the child snips. The material should be thicker than construction paper and approximately 1" in width. Possible materials include modeling clay, straws or laminated strips of paper. (Do not use fabric or yarn.)
- To make the activity more difficult, increase the width of the strips $1^1/_2$" or 2".
- Place sheets and strips of paper of various sizes in a large tub. Then encourage the child to cut and snip the sheets of paper however he or she chooses. After snipping numerous strips of paper, the child may glue the pieces onto a large sheet of construction paper to make a picture.
- Count the number of snips in each strip of paper or classify the strips according to color or length.
- Cut a fringe into a strip of paper and make it into a headband for dress-up. Or let the child draw a picture and cut a fringe around the border for decoration.

Activity 17: Making Pull Toys

Skill areas addressed

✔ in-hand manipulation, visual motor skills

Goal

✔ The child will independently string 8 egg cups to make a pull toy.

Supplies Needed

Empty egg carton (preferably cardboard)

Adult scissors

A thin string, with a hard tip, at least 40" long (Dip the end of the string in glue or wrap it in tape to harden it.)

Washable, nontoxic markers

Instructions

In advance: Cut the egg carton apart into individual egg cups. Cut a hole in the bottom center of each cup (making sure the hole is large enough for the string to pass through easily). Knot the end of the string so that the egg cups cannot slip off.

With the child: First allow the child to color the egg cups in any desired fashion (for example, to make them look like a worm or a train or just random designs). Next instruct him or her to thread at least 8 of the 12 egg cups onto the string, pushing the egg cups all the way down to the knotted end. Make a handle in the tip end for the child. Then encourage the child to pull the toy across the floor and pretend it is a worm or a train.

Activity 17: Making Pull Toys (cont.)

Suggested Modifications and Adaptations

- Provide a demonstration of stringing the egg cups.
- If the child has difficulty, provide verbal cues and hand-over-hand assistance as necessary.
- If manipulating the string and egg cup simultaneously is too difficult, hold the string for the child. After the child sticks the egg cup on the string, demonstrate how to pull the string out the other side of the egg cup.
- If this activity seems too difficult for the child, repeat Activity 1 ("Stringing Medium-Sized Beads") and Activity 8 ("Teddy Bear Lace-up") to provide practice at a more basic level.
- Consult the OT if the child continues to have a lot of difficulty.

Optional Fine Motor or Educational Extension Activities

- Complete the same activity using cardboard toilet paper rolls.
- Complete the same activity with egg cups, but make a necklace instead of a pull toy.

Activity 18: Pegboard Challenge

Skill areas addressed

✔ in-hand manipulation, visual motor skills

Goal

✔ The child will independently place 6 pegs in pegboard by picking up 3 or 4 pegs at the same time using his or her dominant hand and putting them in the pegboard one at a time, using only that hand.

Supplies Needed

6-8 medium-sized pegs (The end of the peg placed into the board should be at least $1/2$" in diameter.)

Pegboard, preferably made of foam

Instructions

Instruct the child to pick up 3 or 4 pegs at once using the dominant hand, then to place the pegs in the pegboard one at a time using only that hand. Encourage the child to use just the thumb and index finger to hold the peg being placed, and to use the other fingers to keep the other pegs in the palm until ready for use. Then the child should use the thumb to move the next peg down the fingers and into position for use. After placing at least 6 pegs in the pegboard using this technique, the child should attempt the activity with the nondominant hand. (It is not required that the child be proficient at this activity with the nondominant hand.)

Suggested Modifications and Adaptations

• Demonstrate the activity.
• If the child is having difficulty, provide hand-over-hand assistance, then fade to verbal cues as the child gains independence.
• If the child is unable to hold 3 or 4 pegs at once with the dominant hand, try using just 2 pegs at a time until the child gains proficiency and confidence.
• If the child is unable to hold and place pegs simultaneously with the nondominant hand, simply have the child place the pegs in the pegboard one at a time, as described in Activity 2 ("Pegboard Patterns").
• Consult the OT if the child remains unable to complete this activity holding at least 3 pegs at once in the dominant hand.

Activity 18: Pegboard Challenge (cont.)

Optional Fine Motor or Educational Extension Activities

- Vary the size and kind of pegs and pegboard used.
- Make a geometric shape (e.g., a triangle, square, rectangle) out of pegs. Have the child copy the design while holding several pegs at once.
- Do a similar activity with coins: Have the child pick up 2 coins at once and drop one in a piggy bank while retaining the other in the palm. If successful, have the child hold several coins at once. Then progress to having the child use the thumb to slide each coin down the fingers when it is ready for use.
- See if the child can name the coins and say how much each is worth.

Activity 19: Cutting on a Line

Skill areas addressed

✔ in-hand manipulation, visual motor skills, scissors skills and grasp

Goal

✔ The child will cut along a 2"-3" line, cutting within at least $1/2$" of the line for at least 4 lines.

Supplies Needed

Child safety scissors

Black marker

Strips of construction paper 2"-3" wide

Instructions

In advance: Draw 4-5 straight lines across the width of each strip with the black marker.

With the child: Instruct the child to cut along the line across the width of the strip. Encourage the child to open the scissors and make a second cut along the line, rather than clamping down on the paper and tearing it. Have the child continue until he or she becomes proficient at the activity or cuts along at least 4 lines (cutting across the entire width of the paper). At this point in the curriculum the child should maintain the "thumb up" position while cutting, rather than turning down (pronating) the wrist.

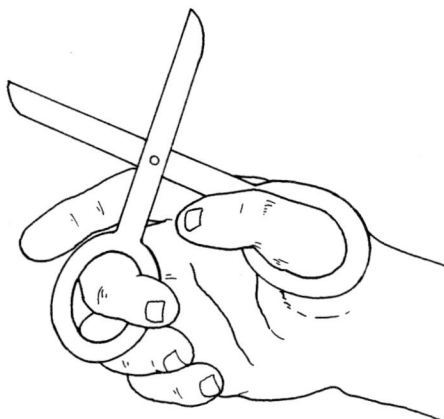

Correct, "thumb up" grasp   Immature, pronated grasp

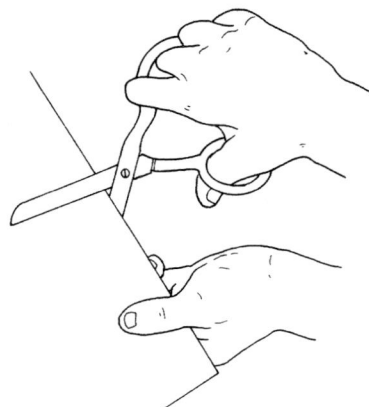

Activity 19: Cutting on a Line (cont.)

Suggested Modifications and Adaptations

- Demonstrate the activity.
- If the child is having difficulty, provide hand-over-hand assistance, then fade to verbal cues as the child gains independence. If the child grasps the scissors incorrectly, provide physical assistance to modify the finger placement.
- If the child is unable to cut all the way across the 2"-3" strips, draw lines on 1" strips for the child to cut. Then when the child gains proficiency and confidence, increase the width of the strips.
- If cutting on the line is too difficult for the child, take one of the 2"-3" wide strips and draw 2 lines 1" apart on it. Have the child cut *between* the 2 lines. Gradually decrease the width between the lines until the child can move to cutting on a line.
- Consult the OT if the child has significant difficulty maintaining a correct scissors grasp.

Optional Fine Motor or Educational Extension Activities

- Have the child cut various types of paper, including thin cardboard, tagboard, construction paper and typing paper.
- To make the activity more difficult, increase the width of the strip by 1" (to 3"-4" strips).
- Let the child use pinking shears to make zigzag lines.
- Draw lines on sheets and strips of paper of various sizes, then place them all in a large tub. Encourage the child to choose different pieces and cut along the lines.
- Take the scraps of paper the child has cut and group them into squares versus rectangles or by color. The child may glue the scraps of paper onto a large sheet of construction paper to make a collage.

Activity 20: Tracing a Cross

Skill areas addressed

✔ in-hand manipulation, visual motor skills, prewriting skills, pencil grasp

Goal

✔ The child will independently trace over 10 crosses with fair to good accuracy (i.e., tracing within $1/2$" of the lines).

Supplies Needed

Washable, nontoxic markers (changeable markers work well, if available)

Writing surface, preferably large pieces of construction paper placed on a vertical surface

Instructions

Using a yellow or changeable marker, make several crosses with lines roughly 2" long on the paper while the child watches. Then tell the child to trace exactly over the lines you have made with a different colored marker. Point out how tracing over the lines changes the color of the crosses. Have the child trace at least 10 crosses. Then have the child attempt to draw some crosses for you to trace over.

Suggested Modifications and Adaptations

- Provide repeated demonstrations and models of drawing a cross, describing the lines as you draw them.
- Hand-over-hand physical assistance may be necessary at first to help the child feel the actions of making 2 intersecting lines. Fade to verbal cues as the child gains independence.
- It is sometimes helpful to pair the horizontal and vertical lines with verbal cues. For example, you might say "zip" as you make the vertical line and "zoup" as you make the horizontal line.
- If the child is having difficulty, it may be beneficial to repeat Activity 5 ("Imitating Lines").

Activity 20: Tracing a Cross (cont.)

- If the child is using an immature or palmar grasp to hold the marker, ask the OT to demonstrate techniques or modifications for facilitating a tripod grasp. Also consult the OT if the child experiences significant difficulty or frustration with the activity.

Optional Fine Motor or Educational Extension Activities

- Repeat the same activity using various materials and supplies:
  Paints at an easel
  Shaving cream or talcum powder on a tabletop
- Make the crosses different sizes and then classify them according to size and color.
- To increase the difficulty, draw other shapes or letters for the child to trace over.

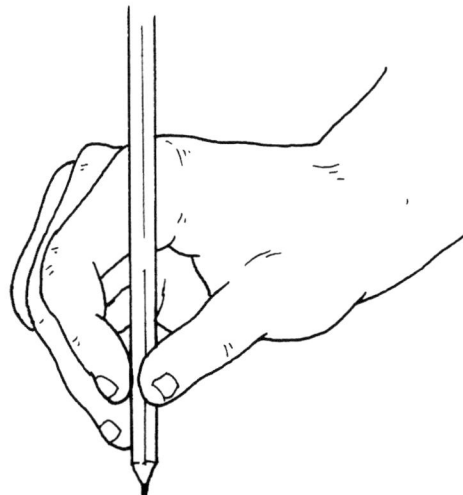

Dynamic tripod grasp

Activity 21: Opening Padlocks

Skill areas addressed

✔ in-hand manipulation, visual motor skills

Goal

✔ The child will independently insert the keys into at least 5 padlocks and turn the keys to unlock them.

Supplies Needed

5-7 key-operated padlocks of various sizes

Keys to fit all padlocks (The keys should be separated from the locks.)

Instructions

Place all the keys in one pile and the padlocks in another. Instruct the child to pick a key, find the padlock it fits and open the lock. Continue practicing until the child becomes proficient.

Suggested Modifications and Adaptations

- Demonstrate the activity, emphasizing how to turn the key in the lock.
- If the child is having difficulty, provide hand-over-hand assistance, then fade to verbal cues only as the child gains independence.
- If necessary, practice using large toy plastic keys and locks until the child gains confidence.
- Consult the OT if the child experiences significant difficulty or frustration with the activity.

Activity 21: Opening Padlocks (cont.)

Optional Fine Motor or Educational Extension Activities

- Repeat the same activity with a variety of types of locks and keys.
- Expand the activity to placing the locks on different toys or objects around the room or house (e.g., the door of a refrigerator or stove, a chair, a table, toy cars) to "lock them up." (Supervise this activity and place the locks out of reach afterwards so the child doesn't inadvertently lock something and lose the key.)
- Hold a discussion about using locks and safety with locks. Name some things that people lock up. Are they valuable things or things that aren't worth very much? What happens if you lock something up and lose the key? Why is it important *never* to lock or shut an animal or person inside something? What could happen?
- Seriate and classify the locks by size, color, difficulty of opening, location or other parameters.
- Place the locks in different locations and have the child describe where they are using prepositions such as *on, under, behind* and *in front of.*

Activity 22: Feed the Hungry Fish

Skill areas addressed:

✔ in-hand manipulation, visual motor skills, prewriting skills, pencil grasp

Goal:

✔ The child will independently trace the dotted lines with fair accuracy (the child's line stays within $3/8$" of dotted line).

Supplies Needed

Washable, nontoxic markers

Photocopies of the "Feed the Hungry Fish" worksheet

Instructions

Instruct the child to help each fish get to the worm by tracing exactly on the dotted line (you can demonstrate by tracing over the line with your index finger). Encourage the child to trace slowly and stay on the line. Make sure the child traces from left to right (fish to worm) rather than vice versa. Accuracy with tracing should improve as the child works down the page.

Suggested Modifications and Adaptations

- If the child is having difficulty understanding the directions, model tracing on one of the lines with a marker.
- If the child is having difficulty staying close to the line, provide hand-over-hand assistance. Fade to verbal cues as the child gains independence.
- If the child is using an immature or palmar grasp on the marker, ask the OT to demonstrate techniques or modifications for facilitating a tripod grasp. Also consult the OT if the child experiences significant difficulty or frustration with the activity.

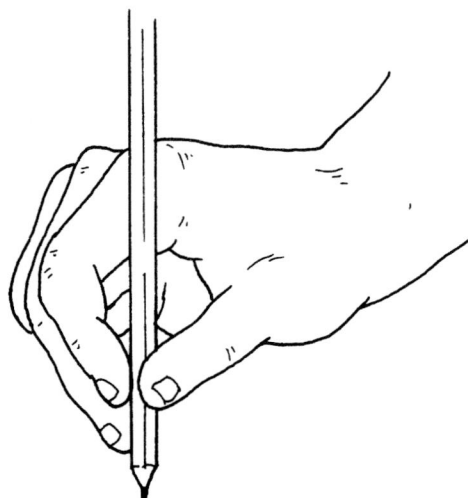

Dynamic tripod grasp

Activity 23: Stringing Small Beads

Skill areas addressed

✔ in-hand manipulation, visual motor skills

Goal

✔ The child will independently string 10 small beads.

Supplies Needed

At least 10 small beads (approximately $1/2$" in diameter with a hole $1/8$" in diameter)

A thin string, with a hard tip, at least 12" long (Make sure the lace is thin enough to fit through the holes. You can tape the end or dip it in glue to make a hard tip.)

Instructions

Knot the end of the string so the beads won't slip off. Instruct the child to string all the beads.

Suggested Modifications and Adaptations

- If necessary, provide a demonstration of stringing the beads. Then have the child take the beads off and string them again.
- If the child has difficulty, provide verbal cues and hand-over-hand assistance as necessary.
- If manipulating the string and bead simultaneously is too difficult, hold the string for the child. After the child sticks the bead on the string, demonstrate how to pull the string out the other side of the bead.
- The child may need to repeat Activity 1 ("Stringing Medium-Sized Beads") and Activity 8 ("Teddy Bear Lace-up") to continue practicing this skill at an easier level. Then attempt this activity again.
- Consult the OT if the child is unable to string the beads.

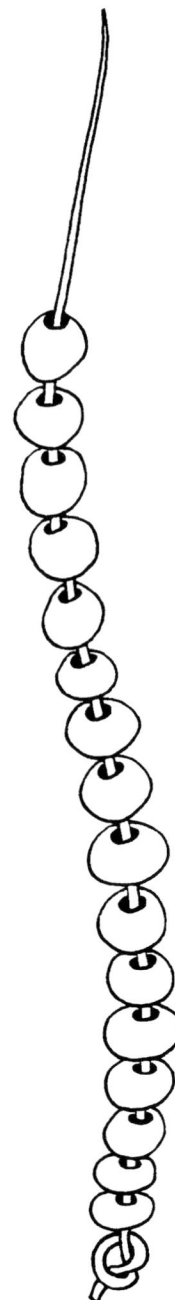

Activity 23: Stringing Small Beads (cont.)

Optional Fine Motor or Educational Extension Activities

- Use the string of beads as a necklace for dress-up
- String a necklace out of cereal loops (such as Cheerios or Froot Loops).
- Use the beads for counting activities by adding and removing beads from the string and counting how many are left.
- Have the child string the beads in specific color or size patterns (for example, 2 yellow, 2 blue or 1 large, 2 small).

The
Start to Finish
Program

Unit 2

Activity 24: Grab Bag

Skill area addressed

✔ in-hand manipulation

Goal

✔ The child will independently identify at least 10 items by feel alone.

Supplies Needed

10-12 small, distinct objects, such as a counting bear, a clothespin, a paper clip, a safety pin, a pen, a marker, a bolt, a small block, a plastic animal, a pipe cleaner and a crayon

A bag, preferably cloth, to hold the objects (Make sure all the items fit into the bag and are not visible.)

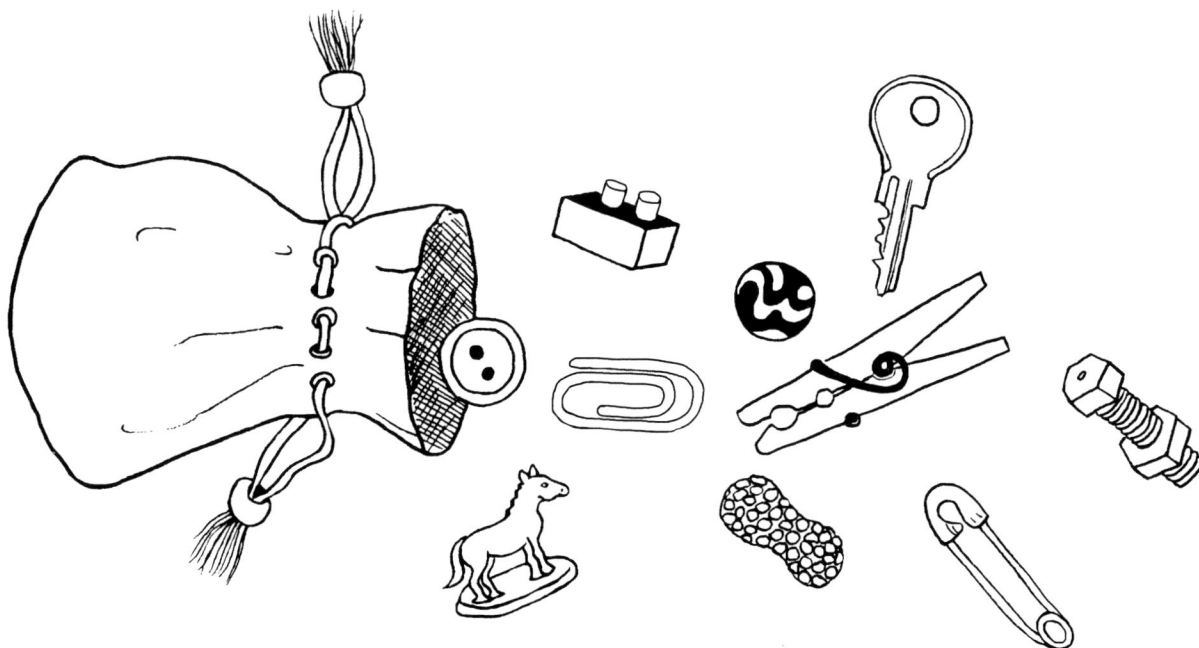

Instructions

First allow the child to view all the objects that will be placed in the bag. Make sure the child is familiar with all the items and can name them on sight. Then place all the objects in the bag. Have the child reach in the bag with one hand and feel an object. The child must guess what the item is before pulling it out of the bag. Continue the activity until all the objects have been removed from the bag. Allow the child to continue practicing until he or she becomes proficient at the activity.

Activity 24: Grab Bag (cont.)

Suggested Modifications and Adaptations

- Demonstrate the activity.
- To make the activity easier, put only 2 or 3 items in the bag. Once the child is able to correctly identify those objects by feel, gradually increase the number of objects.
- If the child continues to have difficulty distinguishing objects, use a few, large, distinctly different objects, such as a plastic cup, an apple and a large building block. Gradually decrease the size of the objects and increase the number of objects.

Optional Fine Motor or Educational Extension Activities

- Vary the type and size of the objects in the bag.
- Count, classify or seriate the objects after they have all been removed from the bag. Talk about the function of each object and where it might be found.

Activity 25: Cutting on a 6" Line

Skill areas addressed:

✔ in-hand manipulation, visual motor skills, scissors skills and grasp

Goal

✔ The child will independently cut on a 6" line with $1/2$" accuracy.

Supplies Needed

Child safety scissors

Sheets of construction paper approximately 6" x 6"

Instructions

In advance: Draw 2 straight, parallel lines approximately 2" apart across the 6" x 6" paper. Use at least 2 sheets of paper or more, if necessary, for the child to achieve success.

With the child: Instruct the child to cut carefully along the lines to cut the paper apart. At this point in the curriculum the child should maintain the wrist in a "thumb up" position while cutting, rather than turning the scissors sideways by pronating (turning down) the wrist.

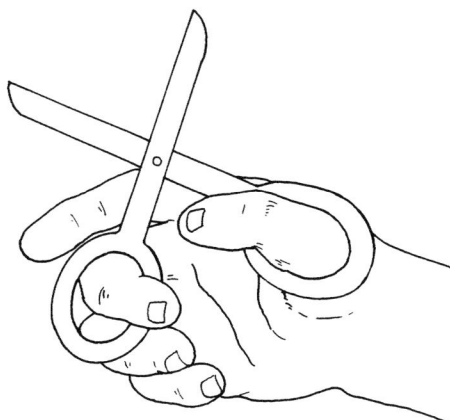

Correct, "thumb up" grasp   Immature, pronated grasp

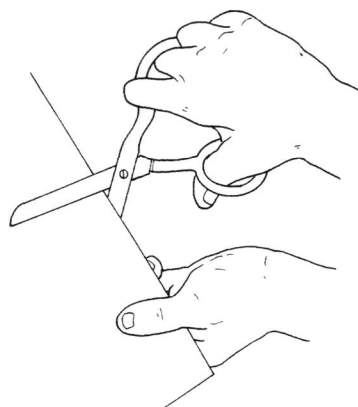

Activity 25: Cutting on a 6" Line (cont.)

Suggested Modifications and Adaptations

- Demonstrate the activity.
- If the child is having difficulty, provide hand-over-hand assistance, then fade to verbal cues as the child gains independence. Provide physical assistance to modify the child's finger placement, if necessary, to achieve a mature scissors grasp.
- If the child is unable to cut all the way across the 6" paper, draw lines on 3" strips of paper for the child to cut on. Gradually increase the width of the paper as the child becomes proficient.
- If the child is having significant difficulty cutting on a line, draw 2 lines 1" apart on a 6" piece of paper and have the child cut between them. Then gradually decrease the distance between the lines until the child is successfully able to cut on a line.
- Consult the OT if the child is having a lot of difficulty maintaining a mature scissors grasp or cutting on the line accurately.

Optional Fine Motor or Educational Extension Activities

- Vary the types of paper the child cuts. Possibilities include thin cardboard, tagboard, construction paper or typing paper.
- Let the child use pinking shears to make zigzag lines.
- To make the activity more difficult, increase the width of the paper the child is cutting across to 8" or 11".
- Have the child draw some lines to cut on.
- Incorporate fantasy play by pretending the lines are roads to houses or stores.

Activity 26: Give the Poor Dog a Bone

Skill areas addressed

✔ in-hand manipulation, visual motor skills, prewriting skills, pencil grasp

Goal

✔ The child will independently trace the dotted lines with fair accuracy (the child's line stays within $3/8$" of the dotted line by the time he or she reaches the last 2 lines on the worksheet).

Supplies Needed

Washable, nontoxic markers

Photocopies of the "Give the Poor Dog a Bone" worksheet

Instructions

Instruct the child to trace exactly on the dotted line from the dog on the left to the bone on the right. (Make sure the child traces from left to right.) Encourage the child to go slowly and stay on the line. The accuracy of tracing on the line should improve as the child works down the page.

Suggested Modifications and Adaptations

- If the child has difficulty understanding the directions, trace one of the lines to demonstrate the task.
- Provide hand-over-hand assistance, if necessary, then fade to verbal cues as the child gains independence.
- If this activity appears too difficult, repeat Activity 22 ("Feed the Hungry Fish") to provide some lower-level practice, then repeat this worksheet.
- Consult the OT for techniques to facilitate a tripod grasp if the child is using an immature or palmar pencil grasp. Also consult the OT if the child is experiencing significant difficulty or frustration with the activity.

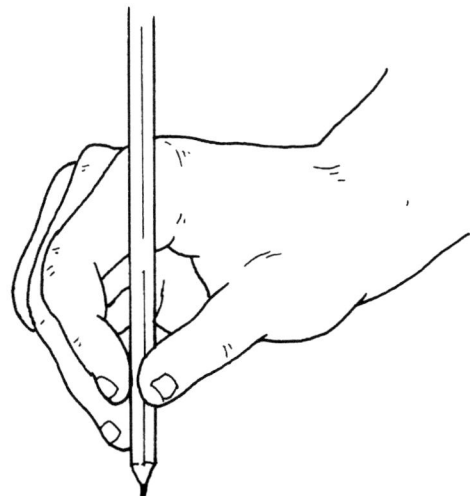

Dynamic tripod grasp

Activity 26: Give the Poor Dog a Bone (cont.)

Optional Fine Motor or Educational Extension Activities

- Have the child trace other path worksheets with simple curved paths. Such activities can be found in many preschool activity books.
- Using a yellow or highlighting marker, draw some curved lines on a sheet of paper. Then have the child trace over your lines with a different marker to change the color of the lines. Encourage the child to try using a variety of markers to see how many different colors can be made.
- While tracing with the markers, systematically try different color combinations to see what colors result. Express the results in a simple equation using the + and = signs: [swatch of color A] + [swatch of color B] = [swatch of color C].
- Let the child draw curved lines with a light-colored marker, then trace over them.

Activity 27: Imitating Crosses (cont.)

- Consult the OT for techniques to facilitate a tripod grasp if the child continues to use an immature or palmar grasp on the marker. Also consult the OT if the child experiences significant difficulty or frustration with the activity.

Optional Fine Motor or Educational Extension Activities

- Repeat the activity using a variety of media:
    Paints and an easel (standing)
    Paper and crayons (sitting at a table)
    Chalk and a chalkboard (standing)
    Shaving cream, talcum powder or
        ketchup (sitting or standing at a table)

Dynamic tripod grasp

- Count the number of crosses made, compare their sizes or group by color. See if the child can draw a series of progressively larger or smaller crosses.
- On a large sheet of tagboard, have the child make several large crosses. Then let the child, or a group of children, extend the ends of the crosses into roads leading wherever they wish (making the roads single lines rather than pairs of lines. Let the children drive around their "city" with toy cars. If desired, the city can be kept in one of the play areas for children to use during free play.

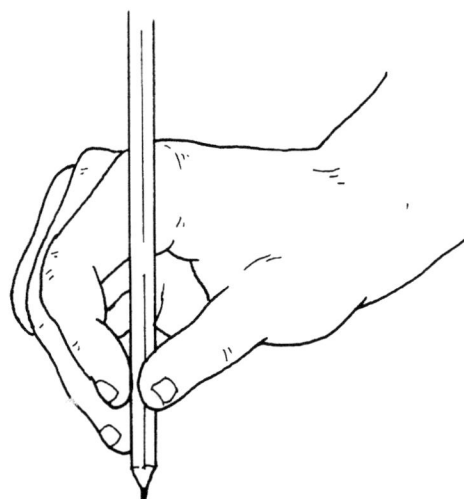

Activity 28: Fluttering Butterflies

Skill areas addressed

✔ visual motor skills, in-hand manipulation

Goal

✔ The child will independently manipulate clothespins and fold at least 3 creases in paper.

Supplies Needed

3 clothespins

A circle, 5"-7" in diameter, cut out of white paper

Markers

Pipe cleaners or 2 matching thin strips of construction paper approximately $\frac{1}{2}$" by 3" (optional)

Glue (optional)

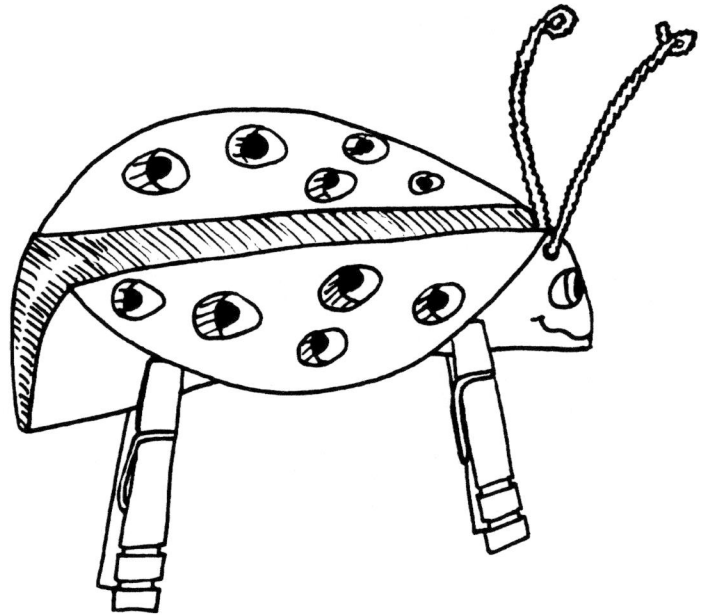

Instructions

Have the child color the circle in any desired pattern, then accordion fold it 3 times, attempting to make 4 fairly equal segments. It is not important that the child's folds be straight or equally spaced, only that he or she makes creases in the paper. Pinch together the 2 center segments on the middle fold, to make the butterfly's body. Hold them together while the child attaches clothespins sticking down from the body to represent legs. (One clothespin in front and one in back will be sufficient to allow the butterfly to stand, or the child can attach 3 to represent the 6 legs an insect has.) The child can glue on pipe-cleaner antennae (or use paper strips) and draw eyes on the butterfly, if desired.

Activity 28: Fluttering Butterflies (cont.)

Suggested Modifications and Adaptations

- If the child is having difficulty understanding the directions, model each step before the child does it.
- Provide physical assistance with accordion folding and opening the clothespins, if necessary.
- Have the child make several butterflies to provide additional practice.

Optional Fine Motor or Educational Extension Activities

- Play a game in which the child picks up different items with a clothespin and drops them in a bucket.
- Have the child place at least 10 clothespins around the edge of a bucket.
- Look at photos of real butterflies. Count the number of legs, eyes and antennae a butterfly has. Talk about the life cycle of butterflies and what they eat as caterpillars and adult butterflies. Let the child wrap his or her butterfly in cotton batting and hang it up with a clothespin on a line to represent a cocoon. Then the child can remove the batting and make the butterfly fly around the room to represent its hatching.
- Read books about butterflies such as *The Very Hungry Caterpillar*.

Activity 29: Catching Some Rays

Skill areas addressed

✔ in-hand manipulation, visual motor skills, scissors skills and grasp

Goal:

✔ The child will independently cut along all the sun rays within $1/2$" of the lines.

Supplies Needed

Child safety scissors

Photocopies of the "Catching Some Rays" worksheet (preferably on yellow paper)

Black marker

Instructions

In advance: Trim off the title and extend the rays to the very edge of the worksheet using a black marker, to assist the child in cutting.

With the child: Have the child cut along all of the black lines to make the rays of the sun. Emphasize cutting all the way to the circle of the sun, but not cutting into it. Encourage the child to cut slowly and follow the black lines exactly. At this point in the curriculum, the child should maintain the wrist in a "thumb up" position while cutting, rather than turning the scissors sideways by turning down (pronating) the wrist.

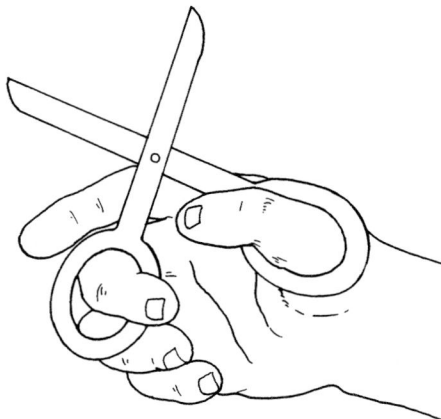

Correct, "thumb up" grasp

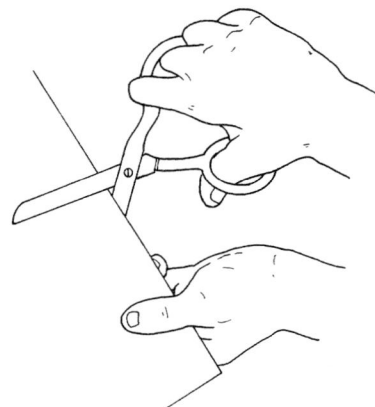

Immature, pronated grasp

Activity 29: Catching Some Rays (cont.)

Suggested Modifications and Adaptations

- If the child is having difficulty understanding the directions, model the activity.
- Provide physical assistance to achieve correct finger placement if the child grasps the scissors incorrectly.
- If the child is having difficulty cutting with accuracy, repeat Activity 25 ("Cutting on a 6" Line") to provide lower-level practice.

Optional Fine Motor or Educational Extension Activities

- After the child has cut the sun rays, hang the sun from the ceiling and watch it "sparkle" as the paper blows.
- Draw 4-5 straight lines across the width of a blank $8\frac{1}{2}$" x 11" sheet of paper. Then have the child cut these lines.
- For a more challenging activity, draw some curved lines across a sheet of paper 6"-8" wide. Have the child cut along the curved lines.
- Incorporate this activity into a unit on weather and what it's like on sunny, cloudy, rainy, snowy and windy days.

Catching Some Rays

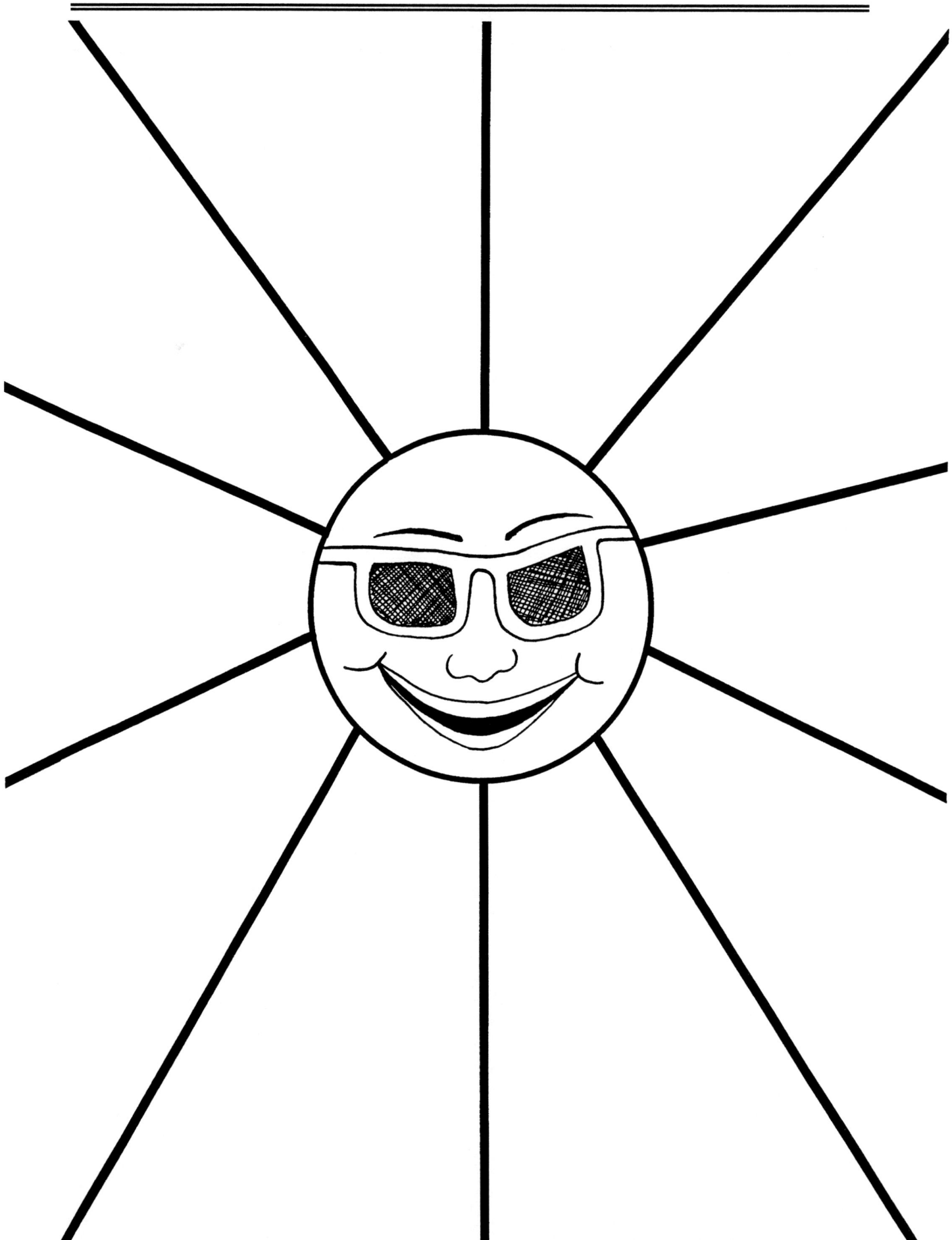

Activity 30: Busy Bee

Skill areas addressed

✔ in-hand manipulation, visual motor skills, prewriting skills, pencil grasp

Goal

✔ The child will independently draw a line through the path without crossing the outer black lines more than once.

Supplies Needed

Photocopies of the "Busy Bee" worksheet

Washable, nontoxic markers

Instructions

Instruct the child to draw a line down the path to help the bee get to the flower. Encourage the child to go slowly and stay within the black lines of the path.

Suggested Modifications and Adaptations

- If the child is having difficulty understanding the directions, complete a worksheet yourself to demonstrate the task.
- If the child is unable to stay within the black lines, draw a path that is slightly curved and $3/4$"-1" wide. Continue making simple worksheets such as this until the child becomes proficient and is ready to attempt this activity again.
- Consult the OT for techniques to facilitate a tripod grasp if the child continues to use an immature or palmar grasp on the marker. Also consult the OT if the child experiences significant difficulty or frustration with the activity.

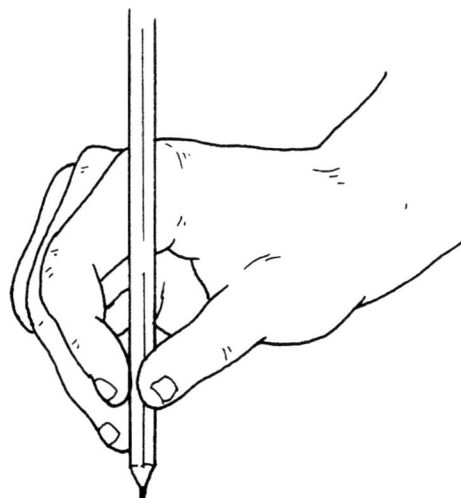

Dynamic tripod grasp

Activity 30: Busy Bee (cont.)

Optional Fine Motor or Educational Extension Activities

- Look for other worksheets with curved pathways in preschool activity books. (Choose worksheets with a single path rather than a maze in which the child has to choose one of several possible paths.)

- On a piece of butcher paper, make up a large curved path for the child to go through with a marker. The child can pretend to be traveling on a road or maybe in a boat down a large river.

Busy Bee

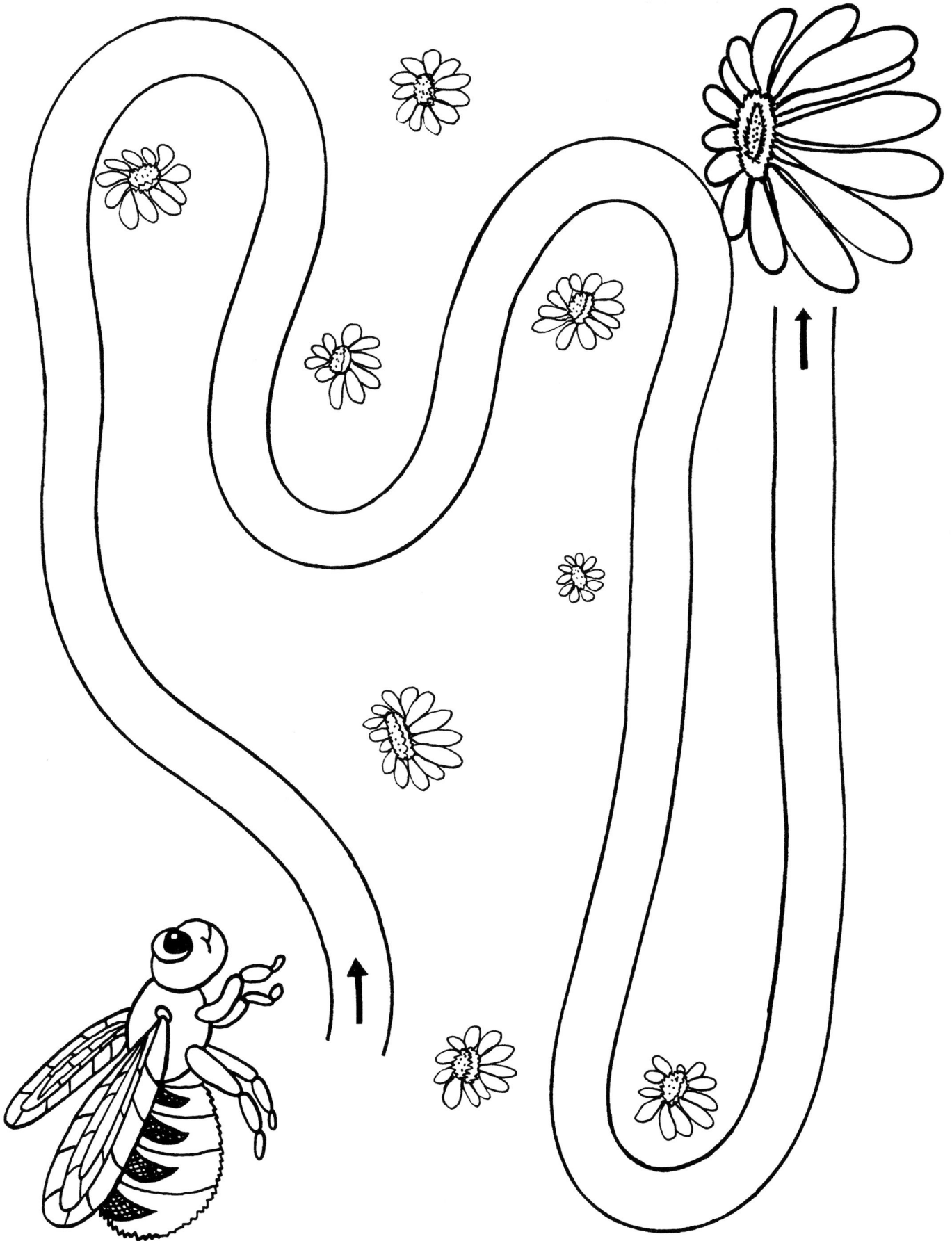

Activity 31: Trace a Square

Skill areas addressed

✔ in-hand manipulation, visual motor skills, prewriting skills, pencil grasp

Goal:

✔ The child will independently trace 3 of 4 squares with fair accuracy (the child's lines are within $1/2$" of the target lines) and will copy one square, making at least one good corner.

Supplies Needed

Yellow washable marker or highlighting marker

4-5 different colors of markers or changeable markers

4-10 sheets of blank paper

Instructions

As the child watches, make 4 squares approximately 2" x 2" on a sheet of paper using the yellow marker or any of the changeable markers. Next instruct the child to trace over the lines you just made with a different marker or the changeable marker to change the square's color. Encourage the child to go slowly and try to trace exactly over the lines you made. Finally have the child attempt to copy 2-4 squares without tracing over any lines. Allow the child to look at a model of a square while working.

Suggested Modifications and Adaptations

- Demonstrate the activity, emphasizing making straight lines and turning corners.
- Continue to make squares for the child to trace if more practice is needed.
- Consult the OT if the child is unable to draw at least one square that has one per-pendicular corner. Also consult the OT for techniques to facilitate a tripod grasp if the child continues to use a palmar or immature grasp on the markers.
- Draw 4 dots for the corners of a square; have the child connect the dots to make a square.

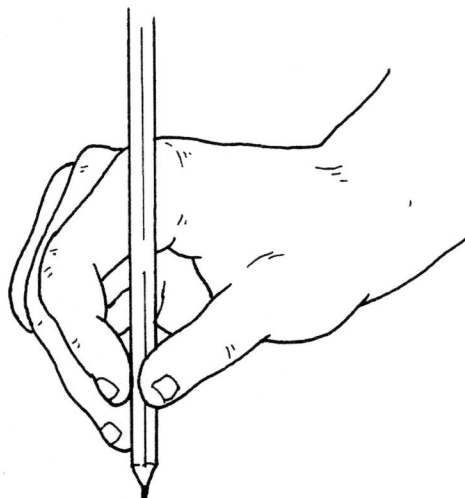

Dynamic tripod grasp

Activity 31: Trace a Square (cont.)

Optional Fine Motor or Educational Extension Activities

- Repeat the activity in a variety of media:
    Paints and an easel (standing)
    Paper and crayons (sitting at a table)
    Chalk and a chalkboard (standing)
    Talcum powder, ketchup or shaving cream on a tabletop
      (sitting or standing)
- Pretend each square is a house and let the child decide who lives in each house (Johnny's house, my house, Grandma's house, etc.). Let the child add roofs, windows, doors, etc. to decorate the houses. The accuracy of the drawing does not matter.
- Go on a treasure hunt around the room, looking for things that are square. See who can find and name the most items.

Activity 32: Tasty Shapes

Skill areas addressed

✔ visual motor skills, prewriting skills

Goal:

✔ The child will trace the shapes with fair accuracy (the child's lines are within $1/2$" of the target lines).

Supplies Needed

Squeeze bottle of tube frosting or ketchup (Single-serving restaurant ketchup packages can also be used.)

Laminated photocopies of the 2 "Tasty Shapes" worksheets

Damp cloth or paper towel

Instructions

Instruct the child to trace over each of the shapes on the page with the ketchup or frosting. (Be sure the child uses his or her dominant hand.) Encourage the child to go slowly and try to stay exactly on the lines. When the child is finished, use a wet cloth or paper towel to clean off the frosting or ketchup. Have the child trace the shapes at least twice.

Suggested Modifications and Adaptations

- Provide a demonstration if the child is having difficulty understanding the directions.
- The child may use both hands to squeeze out the ketchup or frosting if this is too difficult with one hand.
- Provide hand-over-hand assistance, then fade to verbal cues if the child is having a lot of difficulty tracing.

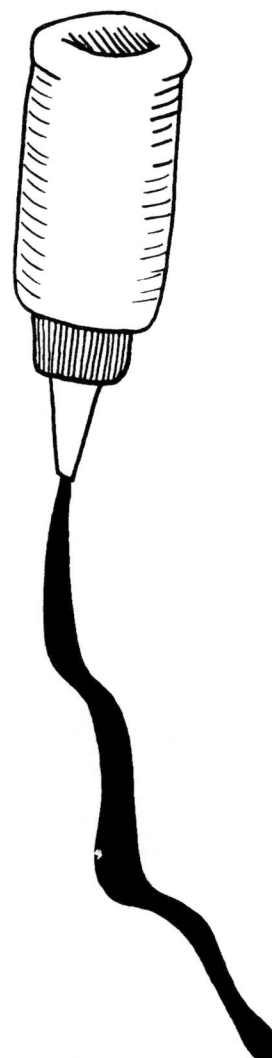

Activity 32: Tasty Shapes (cont.)

Optional Fine Motor or Educational Extension Activities

- Practice tracing the same shapes with a variety of materials.
- Make up large, laminated letter cards and let the child trace over the letters with the ketchup or frosting.
- Have the child practice writing or tracing his or her name with the ketchup or frosting.
- Use frosting to decorate real cupcakes or cookies: place a circle of frosting around the edge of the cupcake or cookie, or draw happy faces.
- Trace shapes or draw pictures using colored glue (mixed powdered tempera paint with white glue). The child may sprinkle glitter over the wet glue to make the pictures sparkle, if desired.

Tasty Shapes 1

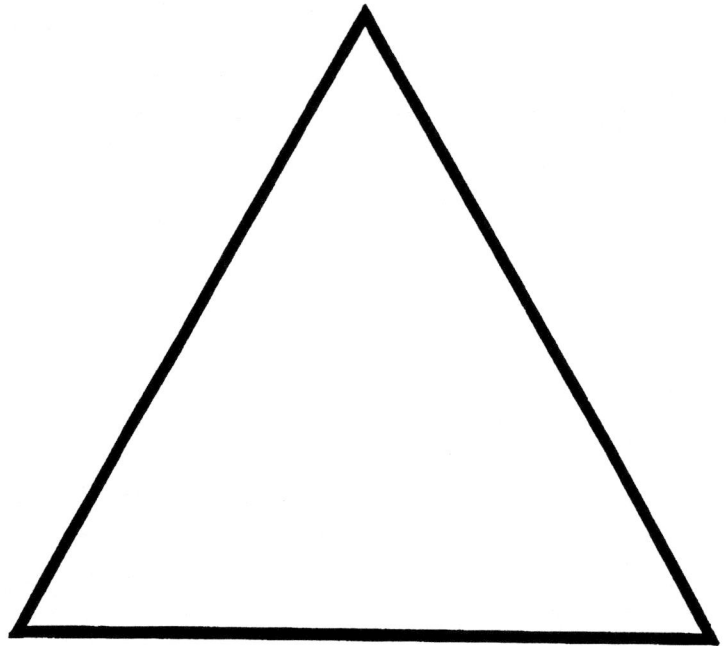

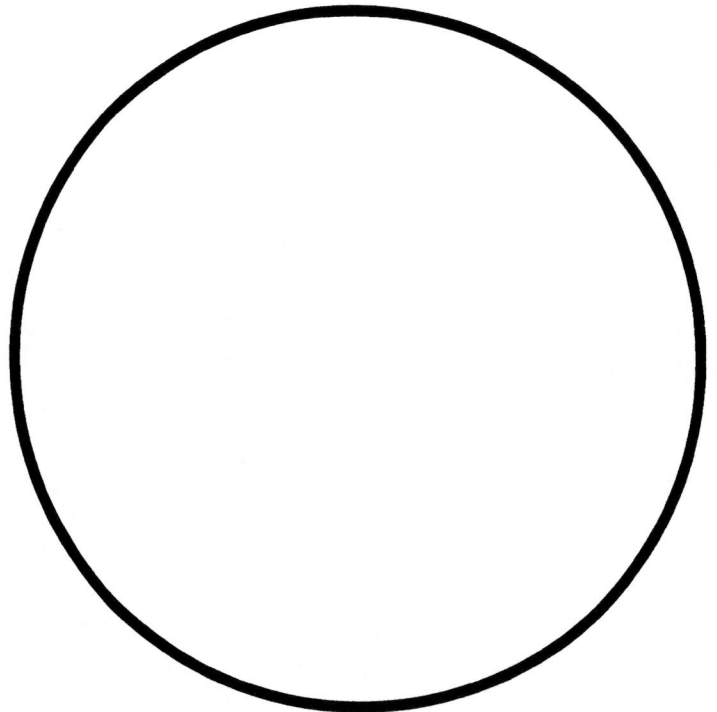

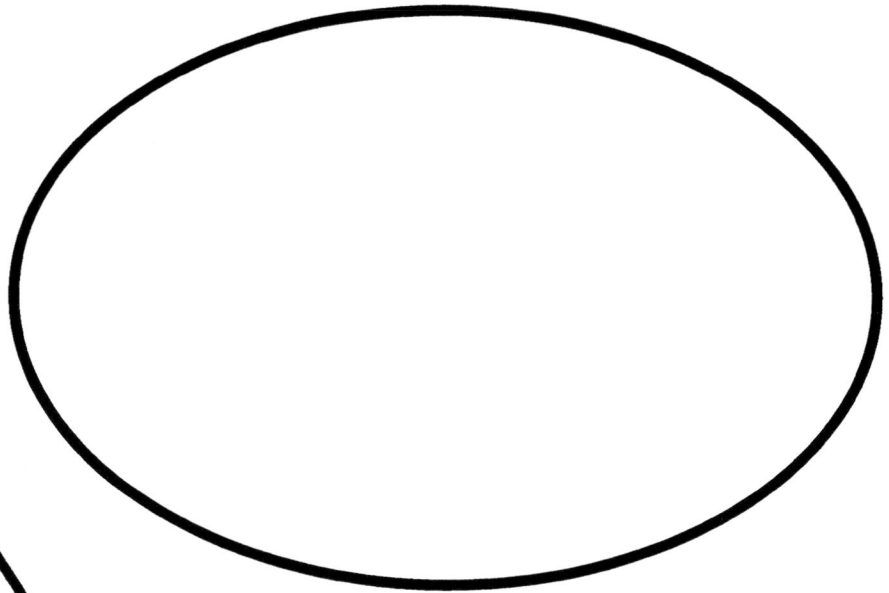

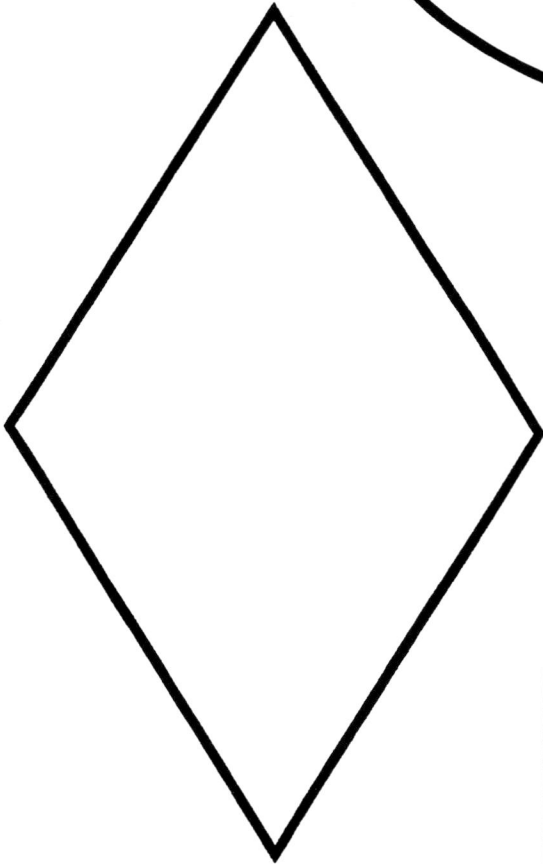

Activity 33: All about Me

Skill areas addressed

✔ in-hand manipulation, visual motor skills, prewriting skills, pencil grasp

Goal

✔ The child will draw a person with at least 5 body parts. At least 3 of the body parts should be recognizable.

Supplies Needed

Chalk

Chalkboard (If a chalkboard is unavailable, use markers and a large piece of paper on an easel or taped to a wall.)

Instructions

Begin by having the child watch you draw a person on the chalkboard. Describe the parts of the body as you draw them: eyes, nose, mouth, hair, arms, legs, hands, feet, etc. Then, leaving your person up as a model, ask the child to draw a person.

Suggested Modifications and Adaptations

- If the child's person is unrecognizable, demonstrate the activity again. Then encourage the child to copy your person.
- If the child still has difficulty, complete the drawing step-by-step. For example, draw a head, then have the child draw one, then draw eyes and have the child imitate those and so on.
- If the child has significant difficulty, provide hand-over-hand assistance, then fade to verbal cues.

Activity 33: All about Me (cont.)

- Consult the OT for techniques to facilitate a tripod grasp if the child continues to use an immature or palmar grasp on the chalk. Also consult the OT if the child is unable to draw at least 3 recognizable body parts.

Optional Fine Motor or Educational Extension Activities

- Draw a person using different materials and surfaces:
    Paint at an easel
    Shaving cream on a tabletop
    Markers on paper at a table or taped to
      a wall
    Frosting or ketchup on a flat, washable surface
- Draw other easily duplicated figures and have the child copy them (sun, train, etc.).
- Incorporate this activity into an "all about me" theme by having the child draw a self-portrait. Provide different colors of chalk or markers so the child can match his or her hair and eye color and draw clothing in favorite colors.

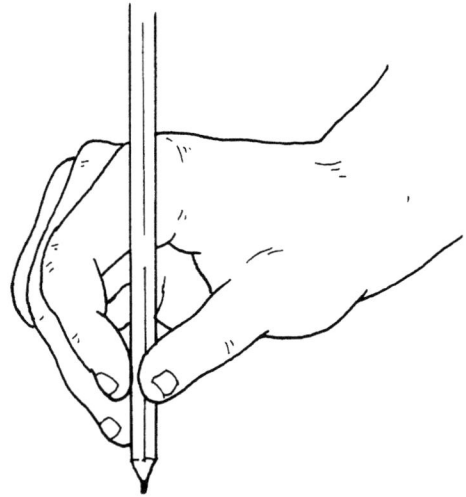

Dynamic tripod grasp

Activity 34: Greeting Cards Galore

Skill areas addressed

✔ visual motor skills, in-hand manipulation

Goal

✔ The child will a fold a sheet of paper in half with the edges lined up within at least $1/2$".

Supplies Needed

Thick construction paper

Washable, nontoxic markers or crayons

Instructions

First demonstrate how to fold the paper in half, emphasizing matching up the edges of the paper and pushing down on the fold with one finger to make a crease. Then instruct the child to fold a sheet of paper in half. Encourage the child to continue to practice folding the sheet of paper, or to fold new sheets of paper, if necessary, to gain proficiency at folding. The child may then color the front of the card with any desired picture or design. Finally, ask the child to dictate a message for you to write inside the card (e.g, "I love you, Mom"). The child can mail or give the card to the intended recipient.

Suggested Modifications and Adaptations

- Provide repeated models and demonstrations of the activity.
- If the child is having difficulty, provide hand-over-hand assistance, emphasizing pushing down on the fold to crease the paper. Then fade to verbal cues as the child gains independence.
- Consult the OT if the child is unable to fold with accuracy or becomes very frustrated with the activity.

Optional Fine Motor or Educational Extension Activities

- Repeat the activity with various sizes and types of paper.
- Encourage the child to fold a new piece of paper as many times as possible. Then unfold the paper and count how many creases are in it.
- The child can make numerous cards to give or send to different people. This is also a good activity for a whole classroom to participate in around a major holiday.

Activity 34: Greeting Cards Galore (cont.)

- What happens when you send a card in the mail? Show the child how letters and cards go inside envelopes. You could give the child a large envelope and let the child draw a stamp on, pretend to write an address, and slip the card inside. If appropriate in your setting, you could have all the children make themselves a card or drawing or pretend letter and place it in an envelope. Write the children's home addresses on the envelopes for them. Then take a field trip to the post office so they can mail their cards to themselves.

Activity 35: Help the Bunny Find a Home

Skill areas addressed

✔ visual motor skills, pencil grasp, coloring, scissors skills and grasp, in-hand manipulation

Goal:

✔ The child will independently cut on the lines with $1/4$" accuracy. The child will color in the bunny holes with fair accuracy (color is no more than $1/2$" outside the circle's edge).

Supplies Needed

Photocopies of the "Help the Bunny Find a Home" worksheet

Child safety scissors

Washable, nontoxic markers

Black marker

Instructions

In advance: Use a black marker to extend the lines to the edge of the page to assist the child in cutting.

With the child: Have the child color in the circles that represent the bunny holes using any desired color of markers. It is not necessary for the child to color in the details within the circle, only to color within the outline of the circles. Then have the child cut on the black lines as far as the circles to show the bunny the paths to the holes. Emphasize cutting all the way to the circle but not into the circle. The child should maintain the wrist in a "thumb up" position while cutting, rather than turning the scissors sideways by turning down (pronating) the wrist.

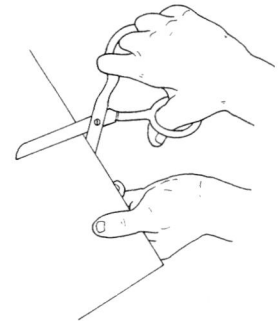

Immature, pronated grasp

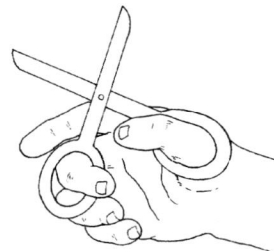

Correct, "thumb up" grasp

Activity 35: Help the Bunny Find a Home (cont.)

Suggested Modifications and Adaptations

- If the child has difficulty understanding the directions, model each step for the child.
- If the child is having difficulty coloring in the holes, provide hand-over-hand assistance, then fade to verbal cues as the child gains independence. Consult the OT if the child is having extreme difficulty coloring with accuracy.
- Provide physical assistance to change finger placement if the child grasps the scissors incorrectly.
- If the child is having difficulty cutting with accuracy, repeat Activity 25 ("Cutting on a 6" Line") and Activity 29 ("Catching Some Rays").
- Consult the OT for techniques to facilitate a tripod grasp if the child is using an immature or palmar grasp on the markers. Also consult the OT if the child experiences significant difficulty or frustration with the activity.

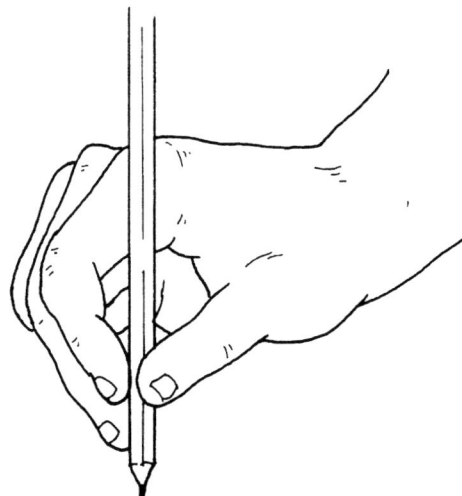

Dynamic tripod grasp

Optional Fine Motor or Educational Extension Activities

- On a sheet of paper, draw some curved lines approximately 8" long. Have the child cut on the lines.
- Draw some straight lines the length of an 8 $1/2$" x 11" sheet of paper and have the child cut on them.
- Draw medium-sized shapes (square, triangle, etc.) on a blank sheet of paper and have the child color them in.
- Expand the activity with a discussion of rabbits: where they live, what they eat and so on. Also read stories about bunnies, such as *Peter Cottontail* or *The Velveteen Rabbit*.

Help the Bunny Find a Home

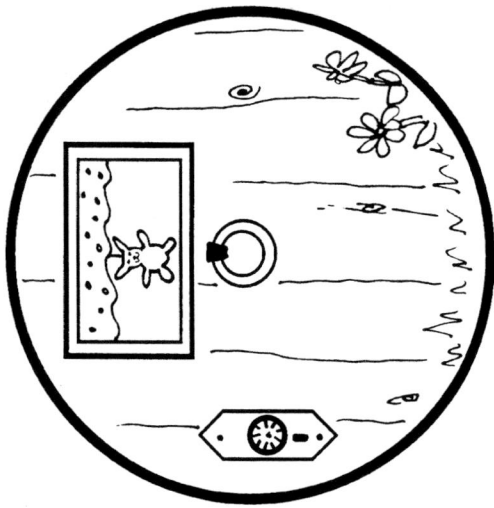

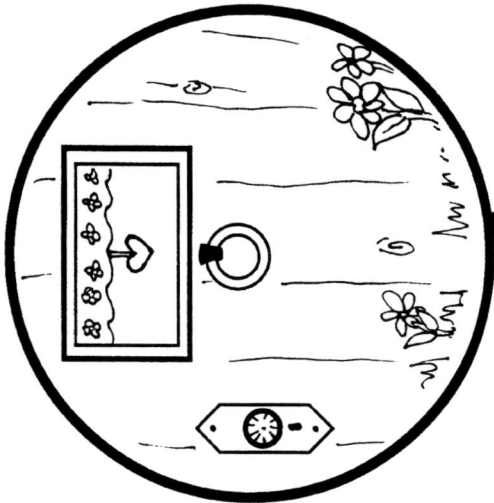

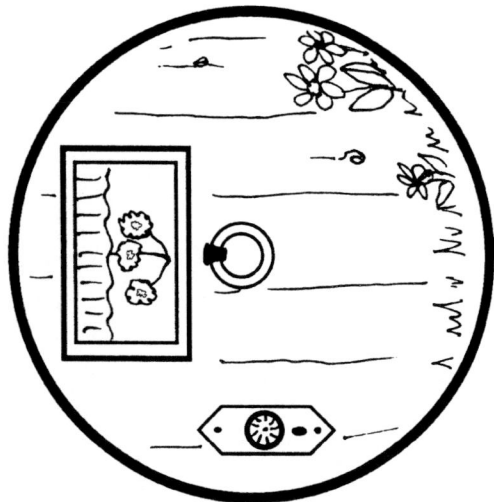

Activity 36: Painted Snowmen

Skill areas addressed

✔ in-hand manipulation, visual motor skills, prewriting skills, pencil grasp

Goal

✔ The child will draw a snowman with 3 circles and a recognizable face. The child will demonstrate an emerging tripod grasp on the paintbrush and marker.

Supplies Needed

White construction paper

Black permanent marker

Watercolor paints and paintbrushes

Small glass of water

Painting smock or shirt to protect the child's clothing

Instructions

Talk about what a snowman looks like. If the child might not have experience building snowmen, you can draw a model. Instruct the child to draw a snowman on the paper with the marker. Encourage the child to add a face on the top circle. Then allow the child to paint in the snowman using the watercolors. It is not necessary for the child to accurately paint inside the circles, but do encourage the child to use a tripod grasp on the paintbrush.

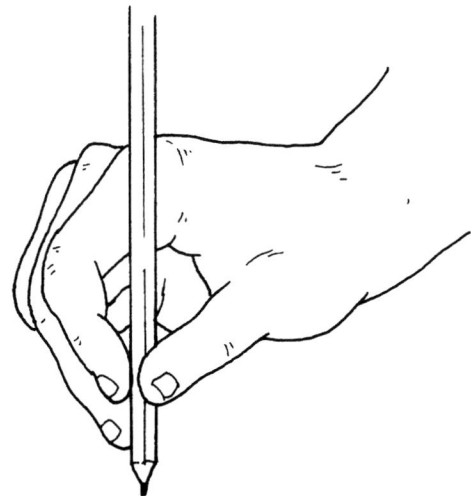

Dynamic tripod grasp

Suggested Modifications and Adaptations

- Draw a snowman as a model for the child to copy if necessary.
- Demonstrate the activity step-by-step if the child is unable to draw a snowman with a model and instructions.

Activity 36: Painted Snowmen (cont.)

- If the child is having difficulty sequencing how to use watercolors, provide hand-over-hand assistance, then fade to verbal cues.
- Consult the OT for techniques to facilitate a tripod grasp if the child is using an immature or palmar grasp on the brush.

Optional Fine Motor or Educational Extension Activities

- The child can draw other simple figures (house, person, etc.) with a black marker and paint the figures with watercolors.
- Let the child use watercolors to color in other simple pictures from preschool coloring books.
- Draw simple shapes and have the child color them in using the water-colors.
- Talk about snow as part of a weather unit. Does it snow where you live? During what season(s) does it snow? What is the temperature like when it snows? What is snow? What color is it? What games are fun to play in the snow?

Activity 37: Help the Spider Get to Its Web

Skill areas addressed

✔ in-hand manipulation, visual motor skills, prewriting skills, pencil grasp

Goal

✔ The child will independently draw a line through the path without crossing the outer black lines more than once.

Supplies Needed

Photocopies of the "Help the Spider Get to Its Web" worksheet

Washable, nontoxic markers

Instructions

Instruct the child to draw a line on the path to help the spider get to its web. Encourage the child to go slowly and be careful not to cross the black lines.

Suggested Modifications and Adaptations

- If the child does not understand the directions, complete a copy of the worksheet to demonstrate the task.
- If this activity appears very difficult, repeat Activity 30 ("Busy Bee") to give more practice at a lower level. Then introduce this activity again.
- Consult the OT for techniques to facilitate a tripod grasp if the child continues to use an immature or palmar grasp on the marker.

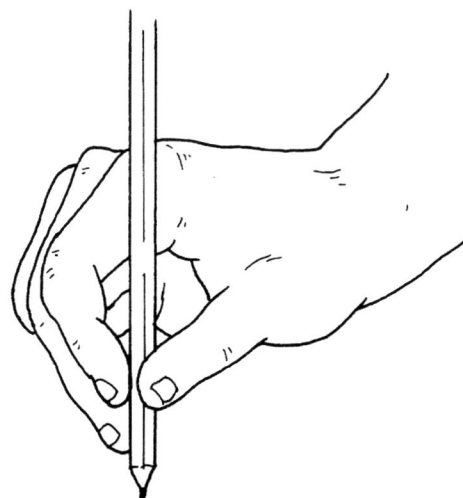

Dynamic tripod grasp

Activity 37: Help the Spider Get to Its Web (cont.)

Optional Fine Motor or Educational Extension Activities

- Locate other mildly to moderately difficult pathway worksheets in preschool activity books. Look for activities in which there is a single path rather than a maze of paths, and the path has gentle curves rather than sharp angles.
- Make up a curved pathway for the child to go through with a marker. The child can pretend to be traveling on a road or down a large river.
- Learn more about spiders. What do they eat? Why do they build webs? How many legs does a spider have?

Help the Spider Get to Its Web

Activity 38: Cotton-Ball Names

Skill areas addressed

✔ visual motor skills, in-hand manipulation, prewriting skills

Goal

✔ The child will use a glue stick to trace the letters of his or her name with fair accuracy (within $1/2$" of the target lines). The child will pull 4 cotton balls apart into at least 4 pieces each.

Supplies Needed

10-15 cotton balls

Large sheet of construction paper (color is child's choice)

Black marker

Glue stick

Instructions

In advance: Using the black marker, write the child's name in large letters on the construction paper.

With the child: Have the child pull each cotton ball apart into at least 4 pieces. Show the child the construction paper and ask what's written on it. Explain that it's the child's name if necessary. Instruct the child first to trace over the letters of his or her name with glue, then to place the cotton pieces on the glue to outline the name.

Suggested Modifications and Adaptations

• Provide a demonstration if the child has difficulty understanding the directions.
• If pulling the cotton balls apart presents difficulty, provide hand-over-hand assistance to help the child feel the required action. Gradually fade to verbal cues as the child gains independence.
• Consult the OT if the child is having significant difficulty coordinating both hands to pull the cotton balls apart.

Activity 38: Cotton-Ball Names (cont.)

Optional Fine Motor or Educational Extension Activities

- Let the child dip the pieces of cotton in paint before gluing them over his or her name.
- Repeat this activity using various names or shapes.
- Let the child glue ripped-apart cotton balls on an animal picture to make the animal furry.

Activity 39: Round and Round

Skill areas addressed

✔ in-hand manipulation, visual motor skills, scissors skills and grasp

Goal:

✔ The child will independently cut out 2 circles with $1/2$" accuracy. Assistance with manipulating the paper and, initially, assistance with scissor grasp may be provided.

Supplies Needed

Photocopies of the "Round and Round" worksheet

Child safety scissors

Washable, nontoxic markers (optional)

Instructions

Instruct the child to cut out all 4 of the circles. Encourage the child to cut carefully around the circles on the black line. Be sure the child maintains the wrist in a "thumb up" position while cutting, rather than turning the wrist down.

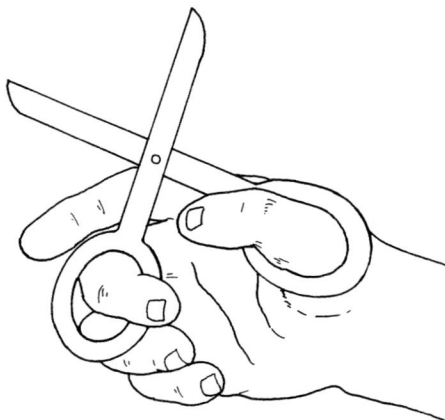

Correct, "thumb up" grasp

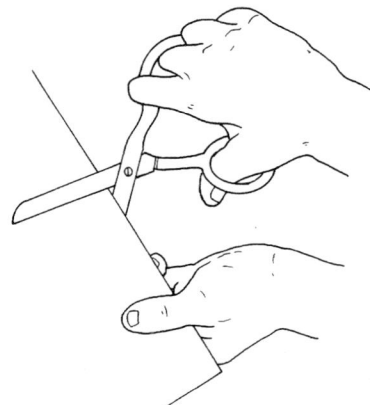

Immature, pronated grasp

Activity 39: Round and Round (cont.)

Suggested Modifications and Adaptations

- Demonstrate the activity.
- If the child is having difficulty, cut straight lines between the circles to separate them.
- If necessary, assist with holding and turning the paper for the child.
- Provide physical assistance to change finger placement if the child grasps the scissors incorrectly.

Optional Fine Motor or Educational Extension Activities

- Expand the activity by letting the child color the pictures in the circles and glue them on another sheet of paper to make a picture. (Do not expect the child to color in the pictures accurately, only to color within the circle.)
- Draw additional circles or have the child draw some on a blank sheet of paper. Make sure the circles are at least 2" in diameter. Then let the child cut out those circles.
- Have the child cut out circles from different colors of construction paper. Then have the child glue the circles onto another piece of paper in a bunch to represent balloons. Allow the child to draw a person holding the balloons, lines for strings to each balloon and any other desired features.
- The child could cut out circles and seriate or classify them by size or color.
- Go on a treasure hunt to find objects that are round or circular.

Round and Round

Activity 40: Large Diagonals

Skill areas addressed

✔ in-hand manipulation, visual motor skills, prewriting skills, pencil grasp

Goal

✔ The child will complete at least 2 left-to-right diagonals (\) and 2 right-to-left diagonals (/) without physical assistance or cues.

Supplies Needed

Large chalkboard (If a chalkboard is unavailable, use markers and a large piece of paper on an easel or taped to a wall.)

Chalk

Instructions

Draw a left-to right diagonal line (in a downward direction) on the chalkboard and identify it for the child as a "diagonal line." Then draw a diagonal line going right to left and say, "Look, here's a diagonal going the other way." Since the task is creating diagonal lines, not X's, make sure the diagonal lines are spaced so they do not intersect. Then erase the lines you have made. Instruct the child to draw large diagonal lines. As always, be sure the child is holding the writing instrument in the dominant hand. The child should complete 10-12 diagonals, then make 10-12 going the opposite direction. The diagonals should be more than 20° off vertical. Encourage the child to use smooth and rhythmic movements.

Suggested Modifications and Adaptations

- Demonstrate the activity again, and leave the diagonal lines up as a model for the child to imitate.
- If the child continues to have difficulty, make 2 dots on the chalkboard at the beginning and ending points of a diagonal and have the child connect them. Then have the child attempt a diagonal without dots.
- If necessary, provide hand-over-hand assistance, then fade to verbal cues as the child gains independence.
- Consult the OT if the child is unable to complete the activity.

Activity 40: Large Diagonals (cont.)

Optional Fine Motor or Educational Extension Activities

- Repeat the activity in a variety of media:
    Paints and an easel (standing)
    Paper and markers (sitting at a table)
    Paper and crayons on a large paper taped to the wall (standing)
    Shaving cream on a tabletop (sitting or standing)
    A drawing toy such as Magna Doodle (sitting)
- Pretend the diagonals are a path or road for a car or bicycle to travel on.
- Show the child a skull and crossbones, railroad crossing signs and other things that have diagonal lines. Let the child attempt to draw them.

Activity 41: Sticky Letters

Skill areas addressed

✔ visual motor skills, prewriting skills

Goal

✔ The child will trace letters with fair accuracy (within $\frac{1}{2}$" of the target lines).

Supplies Needed

5 or 6 20"-24" strands of yarn

Photocopies of the 4 "Sticky Letters" worksheets

Glue (bottle or glue stick)

Instructions

First present the 4 worksheets and see if the child can identify the letters. Instruct the child to trace over the lines of each letter with glue. Then have the child go over the lines again, sticking the yarn to the glue.

Suggested Modifications and Adaptations

- Demonstrate the activity.
- Break the activity into steps and model it step-by-step: Demonstrate tracing one letter in glue and then have the child do it. Then demonstrate placing the yarn on the glue.
- If the child has difficulty squeezing out small amounts of glue, put some glue in a shallow container. Have the child dip the yarn into the glue, then trace over the letter with the gluey yarn. A glue stick could also be used if the child is having difficulty squeezing glue out.
- If the child is having difficulty, provide hand-over-hand assistance, then fade to verbal cues as the child gains independence.

Activity 41: Sticky Letters (cont.)

Optional Fine Motor or Educational Extension Activities

- Write out the child's first name on a large piece of construction paper. Then have the child trace the name with glue and yarn.
- The child can also repeat the same activity using large outline pictures of animals, which can be found in preschool coloring books.
- Have the child match the yarn letters to letters within the classroom (e.g., alphabet flash cards).
- The child, or several children, could trace all the letters of the alphabet in this manner to make alphabet flash cards for letter recognition. (Use card stock or tagboard rather than construction paper.)

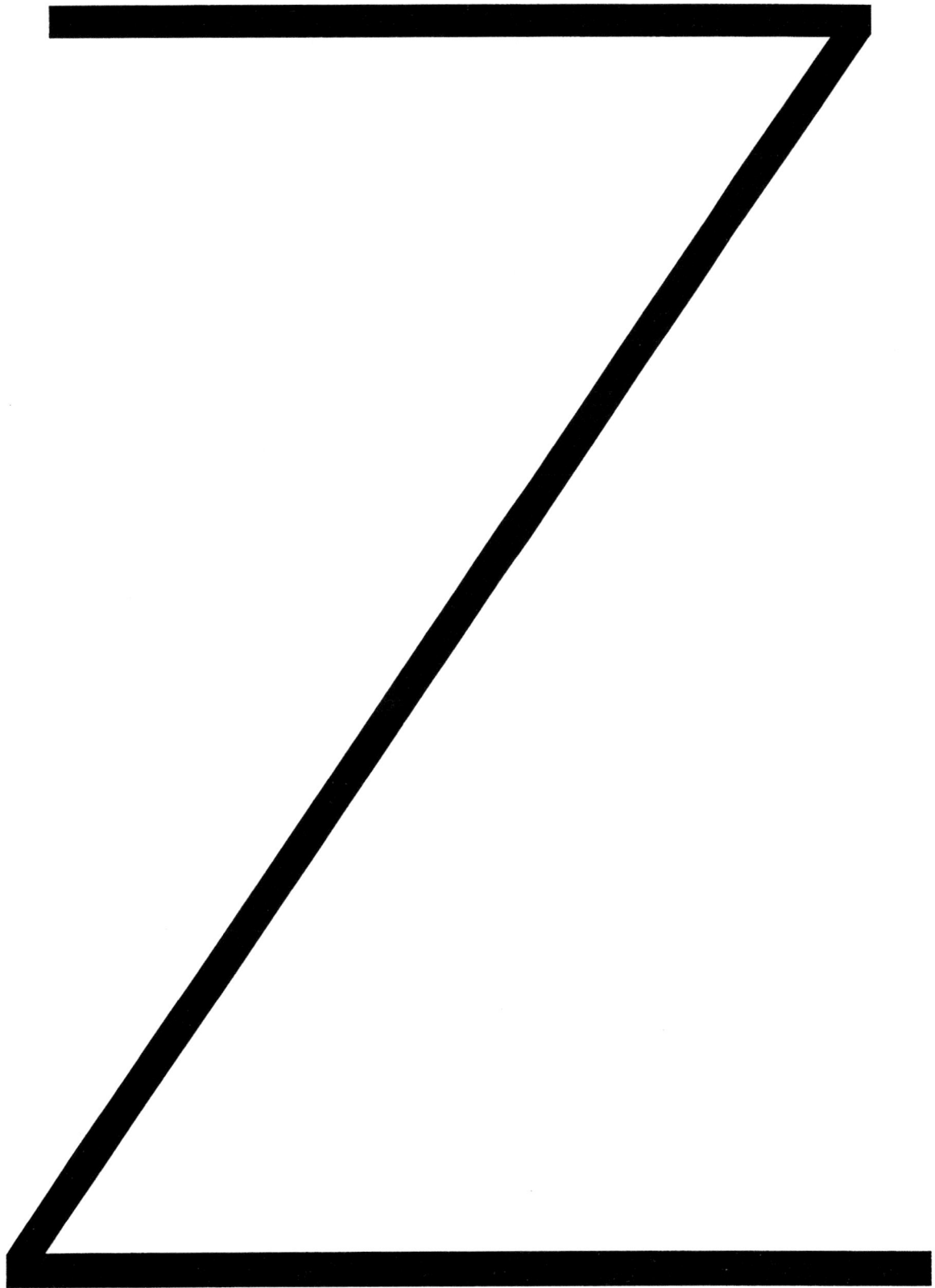

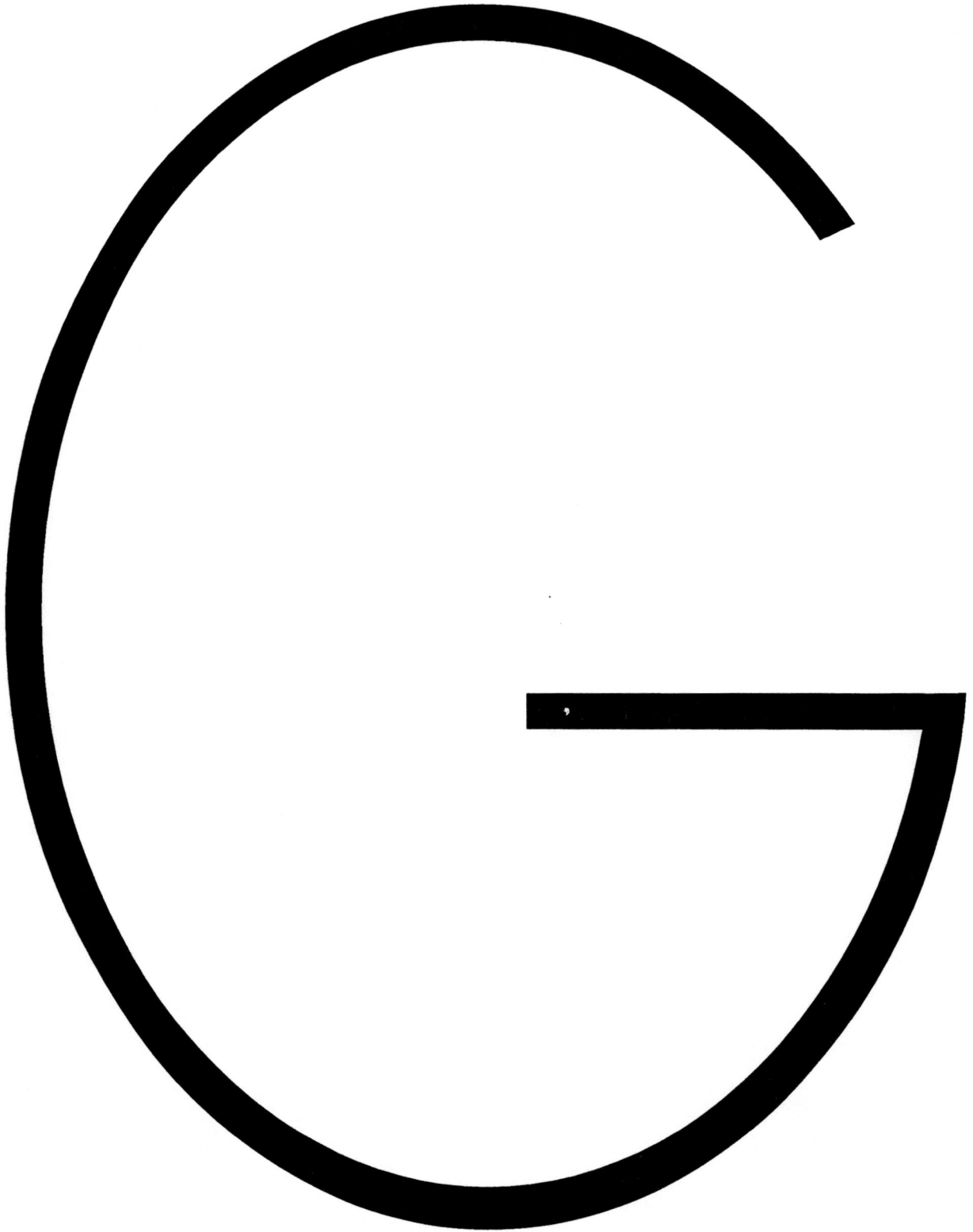

G

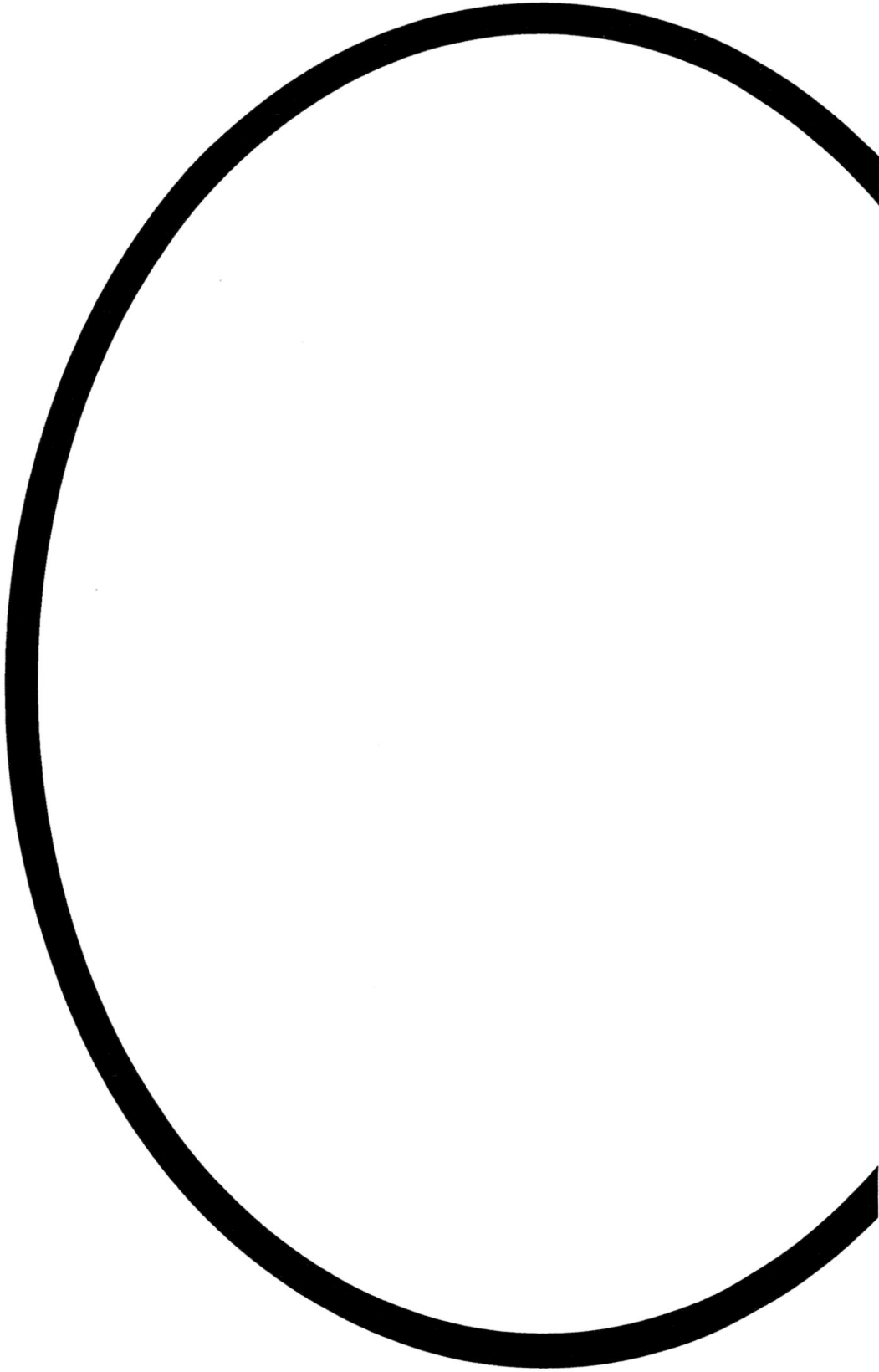

C

122

Activity 42: X Marks the Spot

Skill areas addressed

✔ in-hand manipulation, visual motor skills, prewriting skills, pencil grasp

Goal

✔ The child will make at least 12 X's that have diagonal lines going from corner to corner of the squares.

Supplies Needed

At least 4 photocopies of the "X Marks the Spot" worksheet

Washable, nontoxic markers

Instructions

Instruct the child to make an X filling each square. You can trace with an index finger or provide verbal cues to demonstrate making a diagonal line from the upper left to the lower right corner, then from the upper right to the lower left corner. Encourage the child to go slowly and make straight diagonal lines.

Suggested Modifications and Adaptations

- Demonstrate the activity, stressing the importance of going exactly from the top corner to the bottom corner on the opposite side.
- If the child is having difficulty, provide hand-over-hand assistance.
- Consult the OT if the child's lines are more curved than diagonal, and do not improve with practice.

Optional Fine Motor or Educational Extension Activities

- Draw some X's on a blank sheet of paper or on a chalkboard, then have the child attempt to copy them (i.e., draw more X's using yours as a model). If the child is unable to copy X's, place dots at the beginning and ending points for each diagonal line.
- Draw shapes (triangle, diamond) and letters (N, M, W) that have diagonal lines in tactile materials (such as shaving cream, talcum powder or finger-paints), and have the child trace over them.

X Marks the Spot

Activity 43: Help the Mouse Get the Cheese

Skill areas addressed

✔ in-hand manipulation, visual motor skills, prewriting skills, pencil grasp

Goal

✔ The child will independently draw a line through the maze without crossing the outer black lines more than once.

Supplies Needed

Photocopies of the "Help the Mouse Get the Cheese" worksheet

Washable, nontoxic markers

Instructions

Instruct the child to draw a line through the maze to help the mouse get to the cheese. Encourage the child to go slowly so as not to cross the black lines.

Suggested Modifications and Adaptations

• If the child has difficulty understanding the directions, complete a maze to demonstrate the task.
• If the child is having difficulty with this activity, repeat Activity 30 ("Busy Bee") and Activity 37 ("Help the Spider Get to Its Web") to give the child practice at a lower level. Then introduce this maze again.
• Consult the OT for techniques to facilitate a tripod grasp if the child continues to use an immature or palmar grasp on the marker.

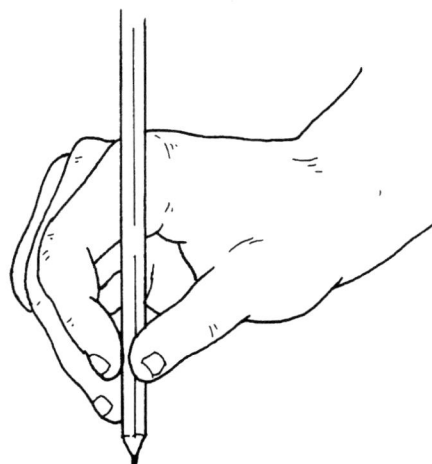

Dynamic tripod grasp

Optional Fine Motor or Educational Extension Activities

• Present other mazes that have 90° corners and in which the main path is easily picked out. Preschool activity books are a good source for mazes.
• Make up your own mazes for the child to go through with a marker. The child can pretend to be traveling on a road in a car or down a river in a boat.

Help the Mouse Get the Cheese

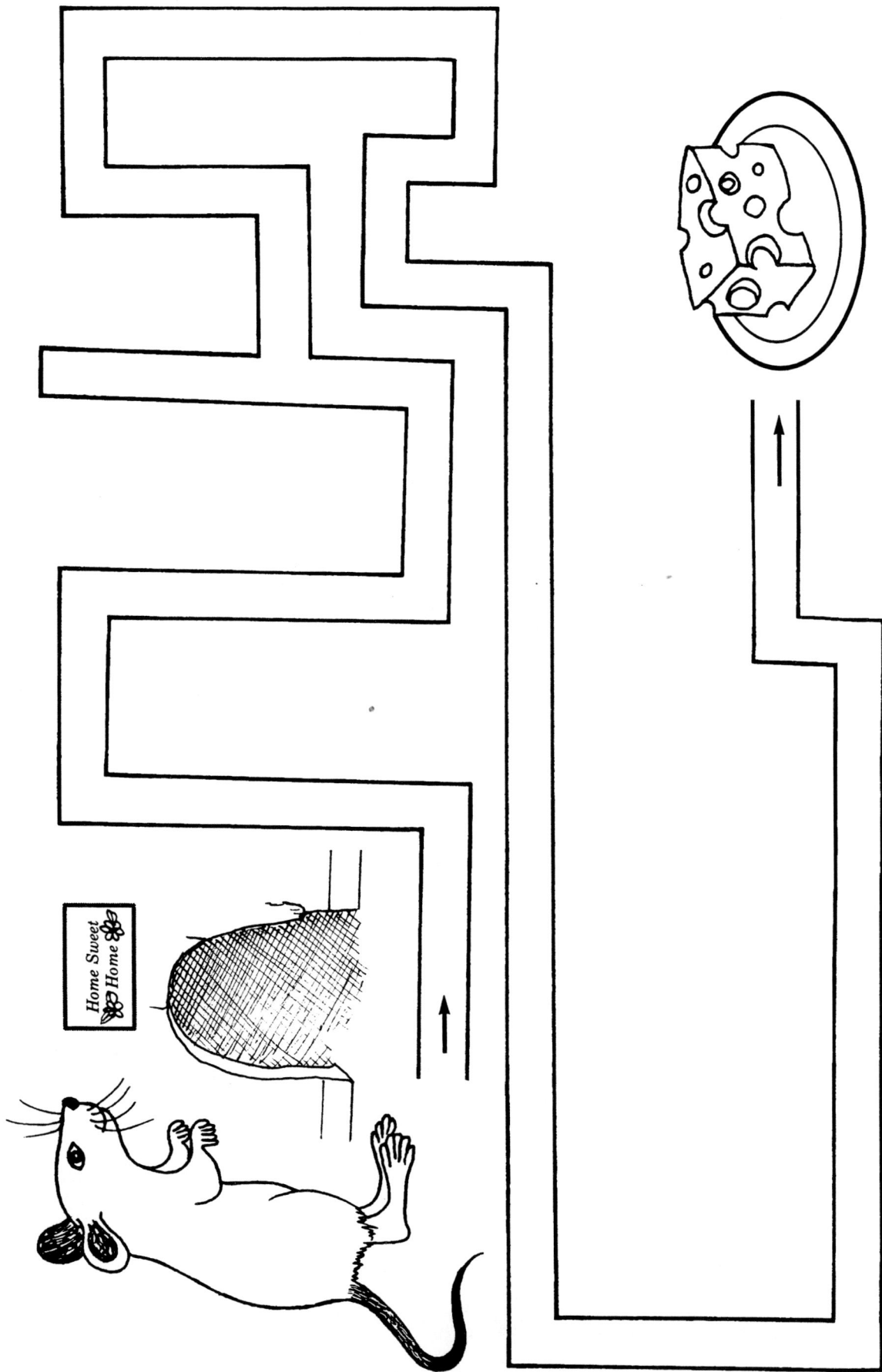

Home Sweet Home

Activity 44: The Accordion Dog, Part 1

Skill areas addressed:

✔ visual motor skills, pencil grasp, coloring, scissors skills and grasp, in-hand manipulation

Goal

✔ The child will color in at least $3/4$ of the dog without coloring more than $1/2"$ outside the outer black lines. The child will cut along the long lines of the dog with $1/4"$ accuracy. (It is not necessary that the child cut around the corners with accuracy.)

Supplies Needed

Photocopies of the "Accordion Dog—Front" and "Accordion Dog—Back" worksheets

Child safety scissors

Washable, nontoxic markers

Instructions

Instruct the child to color in both halves of the dog. Encourage the child to color within the lines as accurately as possible. Next, instruct the child to cut out both parts of the dog, cutting slowly and staying on the outer black line. The child should maintain the wrist in a "thumb up" position while cutting, rather than turning it down so the scissors are sideways. Set both parts of the dog aside for use in the next activity. (If the child has good attention and wants to continue, you can proceed with Activity 45.)

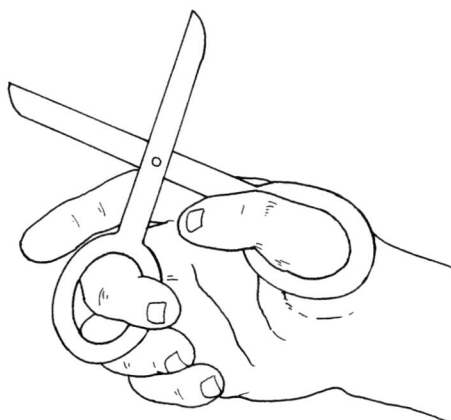

Correct, "thumb up" grasp   Immature, pronated grasp

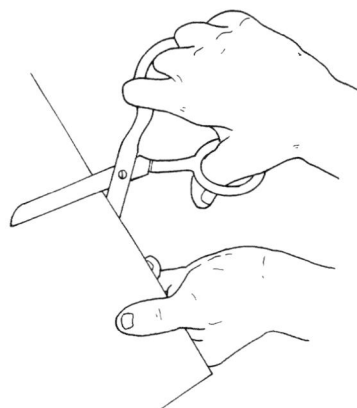

Activity 44: The Accordion Dog, Part 1 (cont.)

Suggested Modifications and Adaptations

- Provide a model of the colored in halves of the dog for the child to look at while working.
- Demonstrate the activity step-by-step, having the child complete each step immediately after you demonstrate it.
- Provide verbal cues as necessary.
- If the child is having difficulty coloring the dog, provide hand-over-hand assistance, then fade to verbal cues as the child gains independence.
- If the child is having difficulty cutting, assist with holding and turning the paper.
- Consult the OT if the child has significant difficulty with this activity. Also consult the OT for techniques to facilitate a tripod grasp if the child continues to use an immature or palmar grasp on the marker. Also consult the OT if the child is unable to cut with accuracy or maintain a mature scissors grasp.

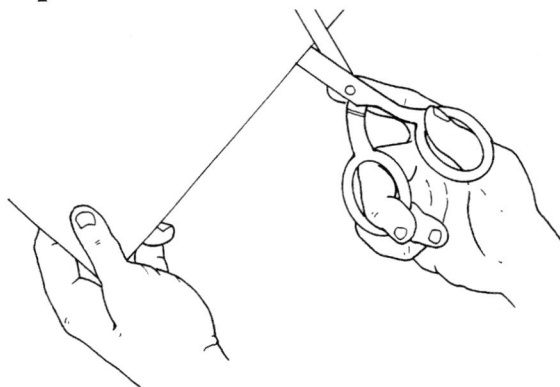

Holding scissors while manipulating paper

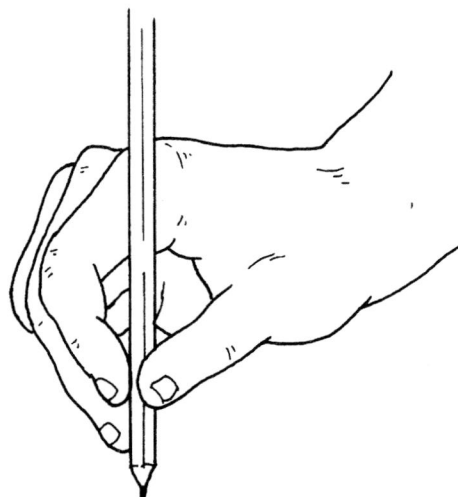

Dynamic tripod grasp

Optional Fine Motor or Educational Extension Activities

- If the child has good attention to task and wants to continue, complete Activity 45 to finish the dog.
- Have the child color and cut out other large, single-object pictures from preschool activity books. Avoid pictures with complex or angular outlines; balls, kites, pumpkins and simple animals are good choices.
- Find out whether the child has a dog or other pet at home (or, if not, what kind of pet the child would like to have). Talk about what the pet likes or would like to do, how the child plays or would play with it and what care the pet needs. Does the child help with caring for the pet? Why is it important to take good care of pets?

Accordion Dog–Front

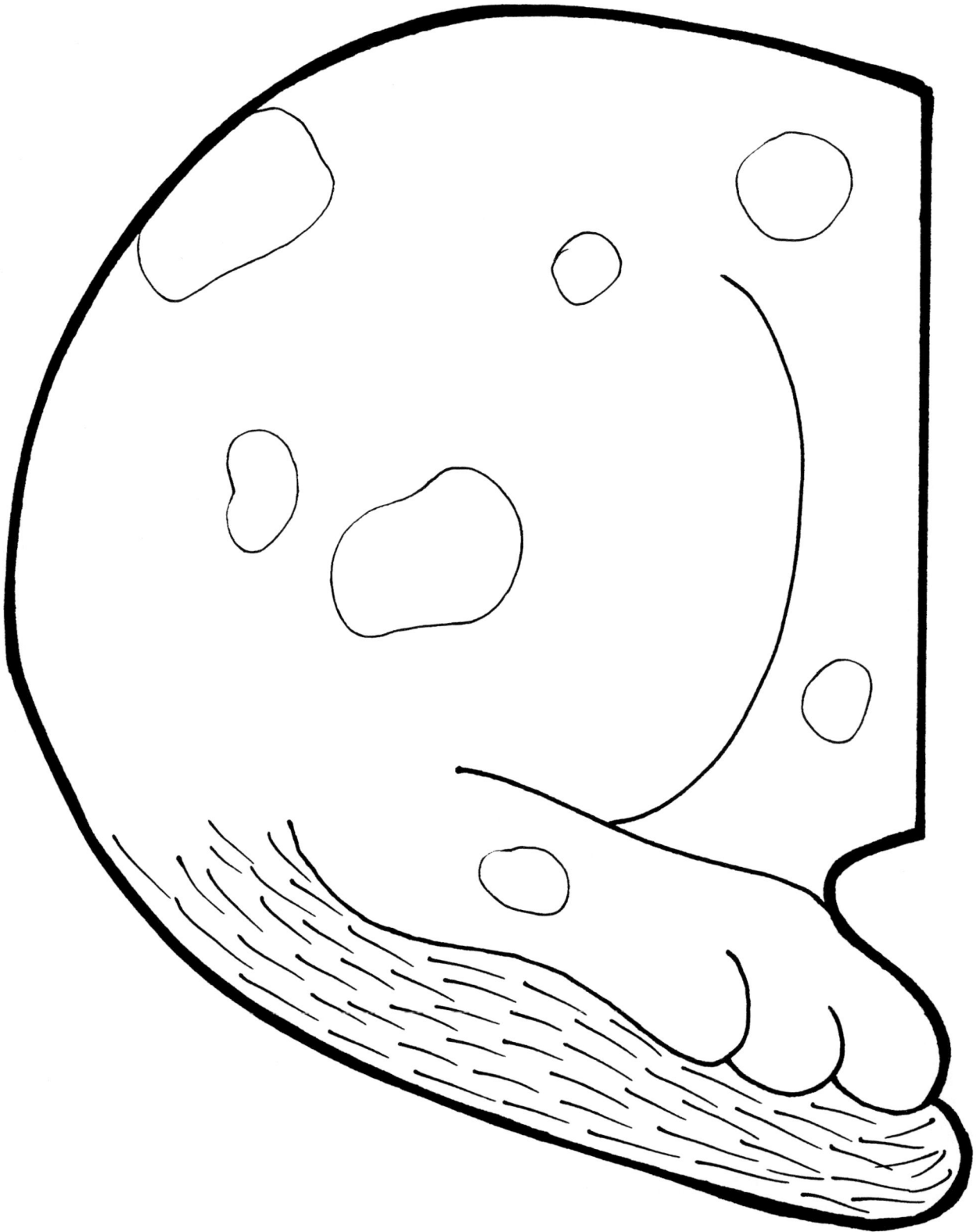

Activity 45: Accordion Dog, Part 2

Skill areas addressed

✔ in-hand manipulation, visual motor skills

Goal

✔ The child will independently make at least 10 accordion folds.

Supplies Needed

Glue

Both dog cutouts from the previous activity

5" x 11" piece of construction paper
(The child can choose the color to match the color of the dog.)

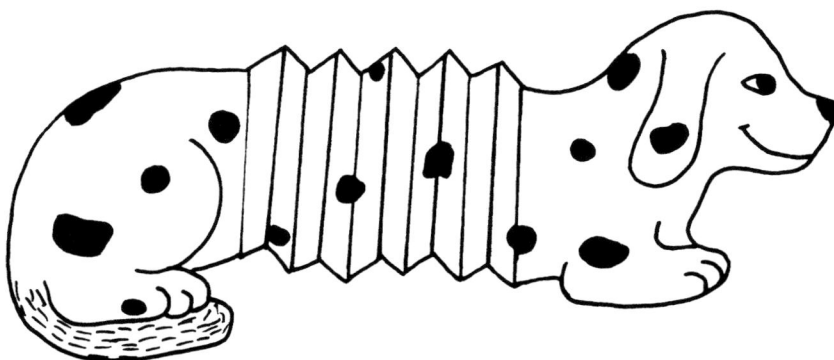

Instructions

Demonstrate accordion folding, verbalizing the entire process. Instruct the child to accordion fold the 5" x 11" piece of construction paper, folding parallel to the 5" side. Make sure the child makes at least 10 folds. Then have the child glue the ends of the folded construction paper to the 2 halves of the dog, so that the paper becomes the middle of the body.

Suggested Modifications and Adaptations

- Demonstrate the activity again, verbalizing each step of the sequence.
- If the child is having difficulty, provide hand-over-hand assistance, then fade to verbal cues as the child gains independence.
- If the child is having difficulty with folding, provide additional sheets of construction paper in various sizes for practice. Or repeat Activity 28 ("Fluttering Butterflies") and Activity 34 ("Greeting Cards Galore") until the child becomes proficient at folding.

Activity 45: The Accordion Dog, Part 2 (cont.)

Optional Fine Motor or Educational Extension Activities

- Have the child count all the creases in the paper.
- Have the child fold long ovals or strips of paper to make worms. Then the child can draw eyes and a mouth on one end.
- Help the child measure the dog with the folds scrunched together and again with them spread out.

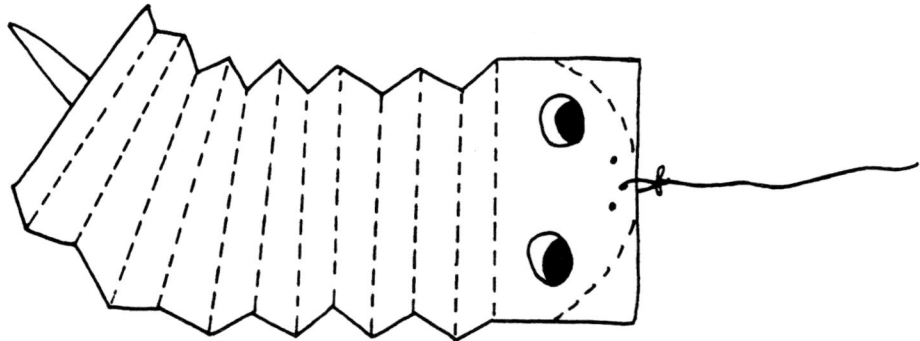

Activity 46: Making a Place Mat

Skill areas addressed

✔ scissors skills and grasp, in-hand manipulation, visual motor skills

Goal

✔ The child will cut strips and slits with $^1/_4$" accuracy using age-appropriate scissors grasp, and will weave paper independently.

Supplies Needed

2 different colors of construction paper the same size

Child safety scissors

Clear shelf paper or laminating material (optional)

Black marker

Instructions

In advance: With a marker, draw straight lines on the paper for the slits and strips. The strips should go across the width of the paper and should be approximately 1" wide. The slits should also be 1" apart but should end approximately 1" before the edge of the paper. It may be helpful to prepare a second place mat in advance, following the instructions below, so the child has a model to copy.

With the child: Instruct the child to cut the first sheet of paper into strips by cutting on the lines. Then have the child fold the second sheet in half widthwise (perpendicular to the slits), with the predrawn "slit" lines on the outside. (This allows the child to begin cutting at the folded edge, rather than trying to start the slit 1" from the edge.) Have the child cut along the marked lines, cutting through both halves of the paper at the same time. Remind the child to stop about 1" from the far edge. The child should maintain the wrist in a "thumb up" position while cutting, rather than turning the scissors sideways down by turning down (pronating) the wrist.

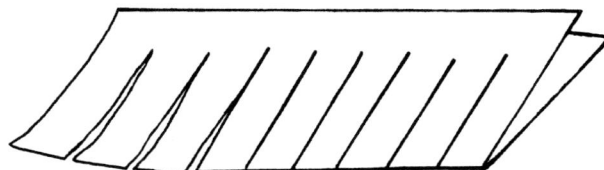

Activity 46: Making a Place Mat (cont.)

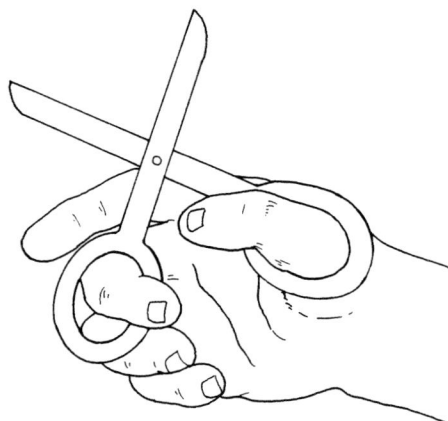

Correct, "thumb up" grasp

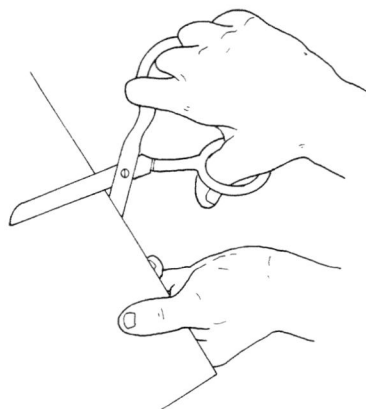

Immature, pronated grasp

Finally, instruct the child to weave the strips of paper in and out of the slits (you may wish to demonstrate this step). The child can use the completed mat as a place mat during lunch or snack. If desired, laminate the mat to allow for repeated use.

Suggested Modifications and Adaptations

- Model each step of the activity for the child as necessary.
- If the child is having difficulty understanding where to end the slits, provide physical assistance.
- If the child is unable to achieve a correct scissors grasp independently or cut with accuracy, consult the OT.

Activity 46: Making a Place Mat (cont.)

Optional Fine Motor or Educational Extension Activities

- Have the child count how many different squares of each color are in the mat. Is there the same number of each color?
- Complete the same activity, but draw wavy lines for the child to cut on to make the strips and slits.
- Make wind socks: cut 10-12 1" strips of paper for the tail and use a full piece or paper for the head. Color the full sheet however desired, then staple or tape it in a circle. Glue or tape the strips on one end for a tail. Punch 2 holes in the "head" end and thread string through for hanging the wind sock.

Activity 47: Snowflakes

Skill areas addressed

✔ in-hand manipulation, visual motor skills, scissors skills and grasp

Goal

✔ The child will independently fold a sheet of paper in quarters, with the edges matched up within $1/4$". The child will cut through the 8 thicknesses of paper with accuracy.

Supplies Needed

At least 4 square sheets of paper, approximately 8" x 8" (White office paper may be best.)

Child safety scissors

String (optional)

Instructions

Instruct the child to fold one sheet of the square paper in half, then in half again the other direction. Then instruct the child to fold the sheet again on the diagonal to make a triangle. Next have the child cut around the outside edges, with any desired designs. Make sure the child maintains the wrist in a "thumb up" position while cutting. After the child has finished cutting, unfold the paper to reveal a snowflake. Finished snowflakes can be hung up around the room as decorations.

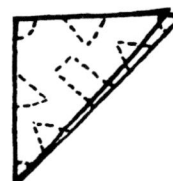

Activity 47: Snowflakes (cont.)

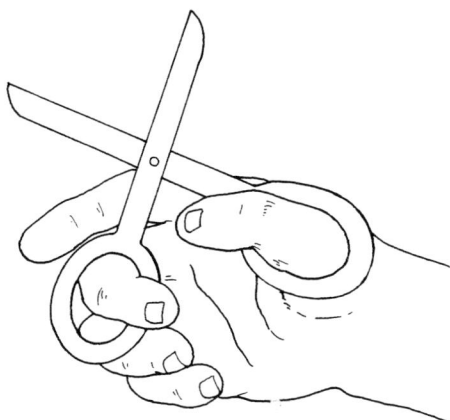

Correct, "thumb up" grasp

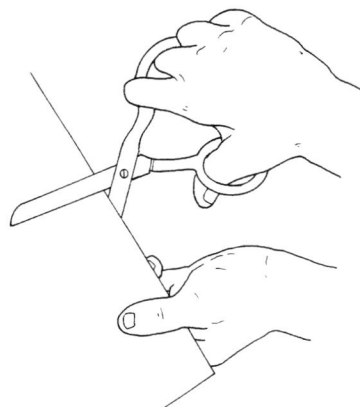

Immature, pronated grasp

Suggested Modifications and Adaptations

- Demonstrate the procedure step-by-step, having the child copy each step immediately after you do it.
- If the child is having difficulty, provide hand-over-hand assistance, then fade to verbal cues as the child gains independence.
- If the child doesn't know what designs to cut in the folded paper, draw lines to cut on.

Optional Fine Motor or Educational Extension Activities

- Make snowflakes with various different kinds of paper:
    magazine pages
    the comics page from the newspaper
    various colors of paper
    tissue paper
- Describe the different attributes of each snowflake (e.g., its size, color, that each is different, the different shapes or designs cut out of it).
- Talk about snow as part of a weather unit. Does it snow where you live? During what season(s) does it snow? What is the temperature like when it snows? What is snow? What color is it? What games are fun to play in the snow?

The
Start to Finish
Program

Unit 3

Activity 48: Memory Game

Skill area addressed:

✔ in-hand manipulation

Goal

✔ The child will pass out at least 10 cards one by one with the dominant hand, while holding the deck in the nondominant hand.

Supplies Needed

Memory card game (If a memory game is unavailable, any deck of cards with matching pairs of cards may be used.)

Instructions

Shuffle the deck. Instruct the child to arrange the cards face-down on the table, holding the deck of cards in the nondominant hand while placing the cards on the table one at a time with the dominant hand. Then play the memory game according to the instructions provided with the game. The important fine motor component of this activity is passing out the cards one by one with the dominant hand and holding the deck in the nondominant hand, so it is not necessary to complete the memory game if the child loses interest.

Suggested Modifications and Adaptations

- Demonstrate dealing out the cards.
- If the child has difficulty passing out the cards, provide hand-over-hand assistance, then fade to verbal cues as the child gains independence.
- Consult the OT if the child shows great difficulty coordinating both hands to pass out the cards one by one.

Optional Fine Motor or Educational Extension Activities

- Play any other preschool card games that require dealing out cards (e.g., "Go Fish" or "Old Maid").
- Have the child sort a standard deck of playing cards into piles of the same number or face card, dealing each card out one-by-one, then placing it in an existing pile or a new pile as appropriate. Once all the cards have been sorted, have the child arrange the piles in order of increasing value.
- Have the child sort number or letter flash cards using the procedure described for the previous activity. (Make sure there are at least 2 cards of each letter or number.)

Activity 49: Jumping Frog

Skill areas addressed

✔ visual motor skills, coloring, prewriting skills, pencil grasp, in-hand manipulation

Goal

✔ The child will independently trace the dotted lines with fair accuracy (the child's line stays within $3/8$" of the dotted lines). The child will color in the lily pads without coloring more than $3/8$" outside the lines.

Supplies Needed

Washable, nontoxic markers

Photocopies of the "Jumping Frog" worksheet

Instructions

Have the child trace the dotted line around each lily pad with a marker, then color in each of these "lily pads." Finally have the child trace the path to make the frog jump from lily pad to lily pad in search of a good home. Encourage the child to go slowly in order to color and trace with accuracy.

Suggested Modifications and Adaptations

- Model the activity if the child has difficulty understanding the directions.
- Provide verbal cues and physical assistance as necessary to assist the child to trace with accuracy.
- If the child is unable to color with accuracy, consult the OT.
- If the child is having significant difficulty tracing or is becoming frustrated, repeat Activity 26 ("Give the Poor Dog a Bone") until the child becomes proficient, then try this activity again.
- Consult the OT for techniques to facilitate a tripod grasp if the child continues to use an immature or palmar grasp on the marker.

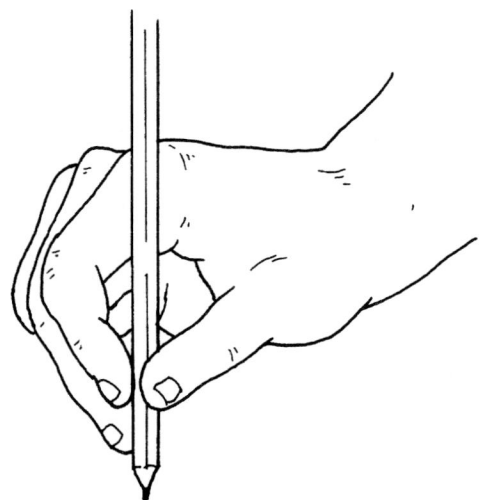

Dynamic tripod grasp

Activity 49: Jumping Frog (cont.)

Optional Fine Motor or Educational Extension Activities

- Using a yellow or highlighting marker, make some curved lines or shapes on a sheet of paper. Then have the child trace over your lines (or shapes) with a different marker to change the color of the lines. Encourage the child to try many markers to see all the different colors that result.
- Have the child draw some curved lines with a light-colored marker, then trace over them with a different color.
- Let the child color in simple pictures found in preschool coloring books.
- Look at photos of frogs and learn about them. Where do they live? What do they eat? How do they move around?

Jumping Frog

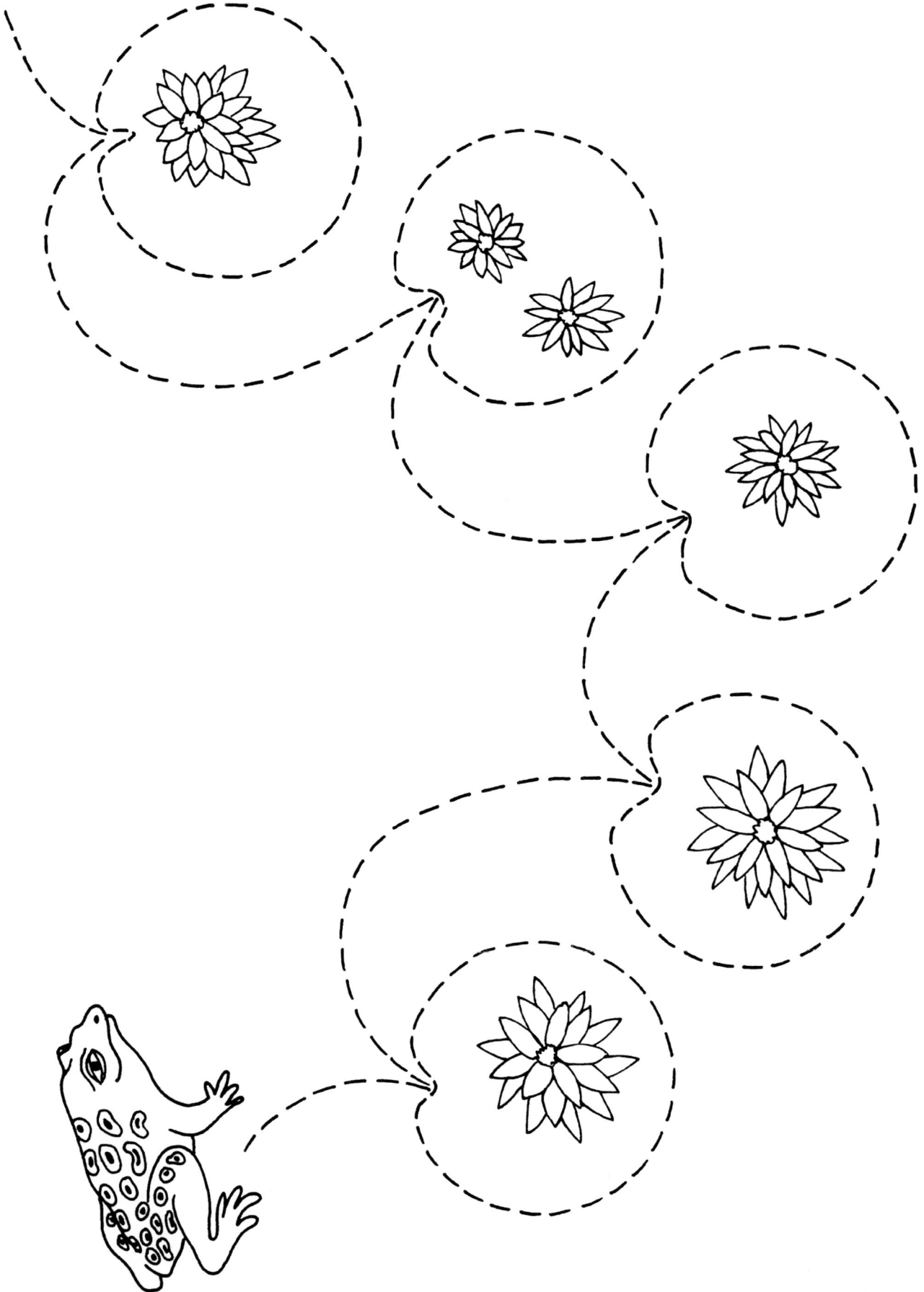

Activity 50: Small-Button Button-Up

Skill areas addressed

✔ in-hand manipulation, visual motor skills

Goal

✔ The child will independently button and unbutton 3 buttons $1/2$" in diameter.

Supplies Needed

Buttoning board or vest that has 3 or more $1/2$" buttons (You could use a shirt or jacket with at least $31/2$" buttons or make a homemade buttoning board by sewing buttons and buttonholes onto a piece of fabric.)

Instructions

Instruct the child to button at least 3 buttons, then unbutton them again. Encourage the child to practice buttoning and unbuttoning until he or she becomes proficient.

Suggested Modifications and Adaptations

- Provide repeated demonstrations and models of how to button and unbutton.
- If the child is having difficulty, provide hand-over-hand assistance to pull the buttons through the holes; fade to verbal cues as the child gains independence.
- To simplify the activity, place the buttons halfway through the holes, then have the child simply pull them the rest of the way through.
- If the child is having significant difficulty and becoming frustrated, repeat Activity 11 ("Big-Button Button-Up") until the child becomes proficient enough to try the small buttons again.
- Consult the OT if the child is unable to manipulate the buttons.

Optional Fine Motor or Educational Extension Activities

- Vary the size and types of buttons used.
- Have the child put on a jacket, vest or shirt with buttons, then practice buttoning and unbuttoning it while wearing it.
- Provide dress-up clothes or doll's clothes that have a variety of buttons and other fasteners for children to use in free play.
- Have the child think of as many different kinds of clothing that have buttons as possible.

Activity 51: The Skunk's Trail

Skill areas addressed

✔ visual motor skills, prewriting skills, pencil grasp, in-hand manipulation, coloring

Goal

✔ The child will independently trace the dotted lines with fair accuracy (the child's line stays within $3/8$" of the dotted lines). The child will color in the squares without coloring more than $3/8$" outside the lines.

Supplies Needed

Photocopies of the "Skunk's Trail" worksheet

Washable, nontoxic markers

Instructions

First instruct the child to trace the dotted lines of each square, then color in the squares for the skunk to stop at. It is not expected that the child will color in the flowers with accuracy, only that he or she will color within the squares. Then instruct the child to trace the dotted line to make the trail that the skunk walks on to get from square to square and smell the flowers. Encourage the child to work slowly in order to color and trace with accuracy.

Suggested Modifications and Adaptations

• Model the activity if the child is having difficulty understanding the directions.
• Provide verbal cues and hand-over-hand assistance as necessary.
• Encourage the child to repeat the activity, if necessary, until he or she can trace with $3/8$" accuracy and color in the squares with approximately $3/8$" accuracy.
• If the child is unable to color or trace with accuracy, consult the OT. Also consult the OT for techniques to facilitate a tripod grasp if the child continues to use an immature or palmar grasp on the marker.

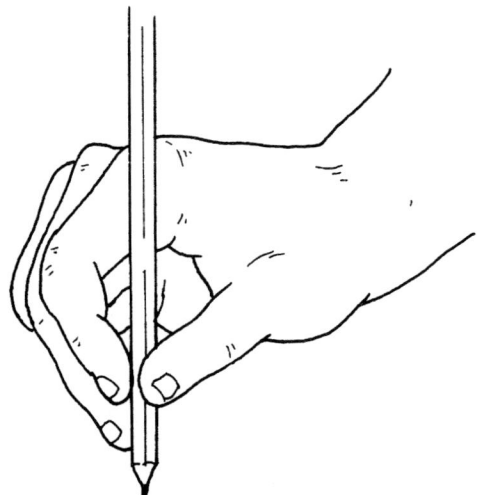

Dynamic tripod grasp

Activity 51: The Skunk's Trail (cont.)

Optional Fine Motor or Educational Extension Activities

- Using a yellow or highlighting marker, make some curved lines or shapes on a sheet of paper. Then have the child trace over your lines (or shapes) with a different marker to change the color of the lines. Encourage the child to try many markers to see all the different colors that result.
- Let the child draw some curved lines or shapes with a light-colored marker, then trace over them with a different color.
- Let the child color in simple pictures found in preschool coloring books.
- Have a discussion about skunks while you are completing the activity. What do they eat? Where do they live? How do they defend themselves against other animals?

The Skunk's Trail

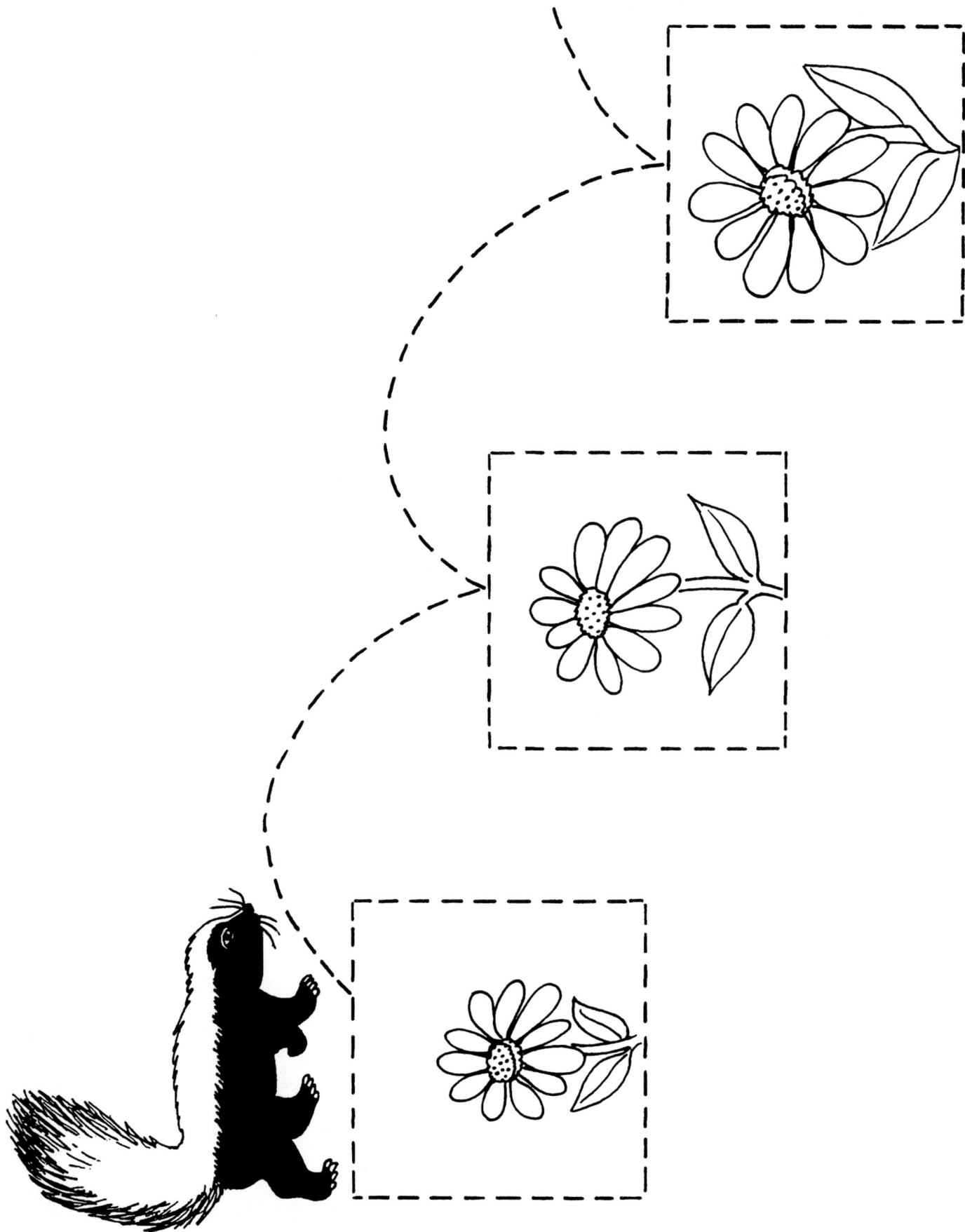

Activity 52: Monkey Business

Skill areas addressed

✔ visual motor control, prewriting skills, pencil grasp, in-hand manipulation

Goal

✔ The child will independently trace the dotted lines with fair accuracy (the child's line stays within $3/8$" of the dotted lines).

Supplies Needed

Washable, nontoxic markers

Photocopies of the "Monkey Business" worksheet

Instructions

Instruct the child to trace exactly on the dotted line from the monkey on the left to the banana on the right, to help the monkey get the banana. Encourage the child to go slowly and stay on the line. Make sure the child traces from left to right.

Suggested Modifications and Adaptations

- If the child is having difficulty understanding the directions, trace over one of the lines to demonstrate the task.
- Repeat Activity 49 ("Jumping Frog") and Activity 51 ("The Skunk's Trail") to provide lower-level practice if the child is having difficulty tracing with accuracy.
- Consult the OT for techniques to facilitate a tripod grasp if the child continues to use an immature or palmar grasp on the marker.

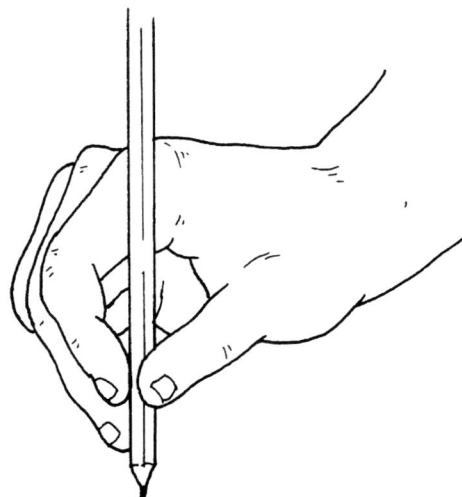

Dynamic tripod grasp

Activity 52: Monkey Business (cont.)

Optional Fine Motor or Educational Extension Activities

- Have the child trace other complex dotted-line paths with several curves. Look in preschool activity books for such worksheets.
- Using a light-colored marker, make some curved lines on a sheet of paper. Then have the child trace over your lines with a different marker to change the color of the lines. Encourage the child to try many markers to see all the different colors that result.
- Let the child draw some curved lines with a light-colored marker, then trace over them with a different color.
- Have a discussion about monkeys. What do they usually eat? Where do they live? What do they look like?

Monkey Business

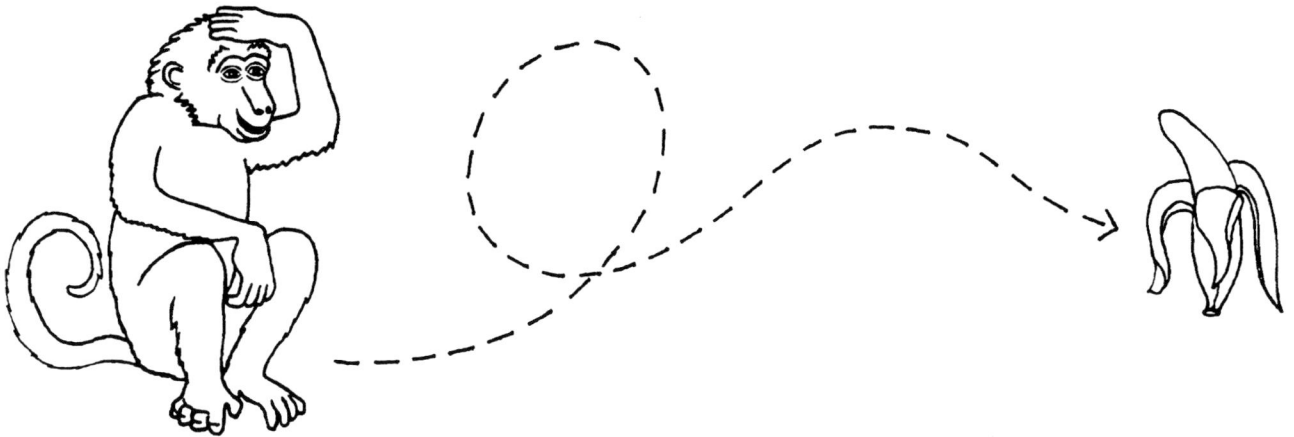

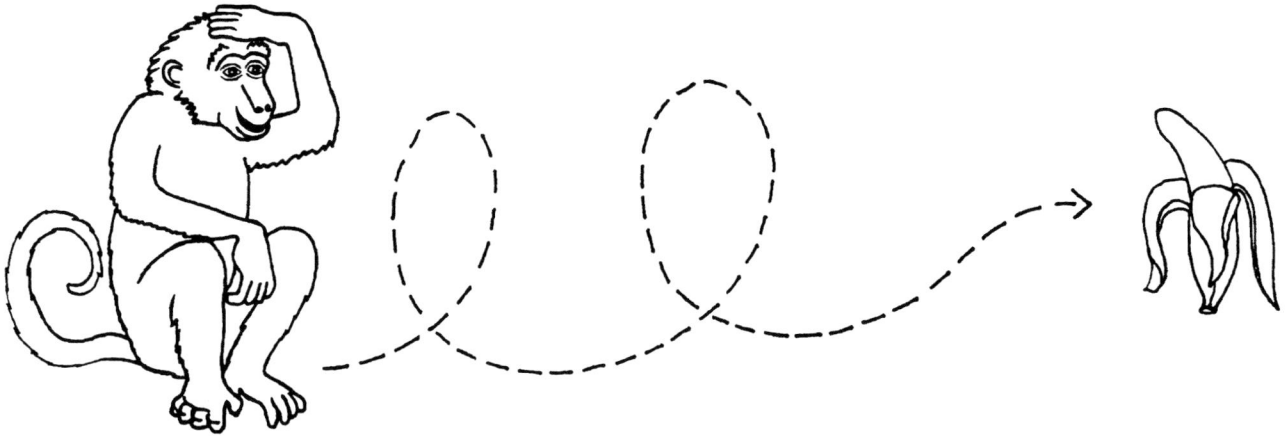

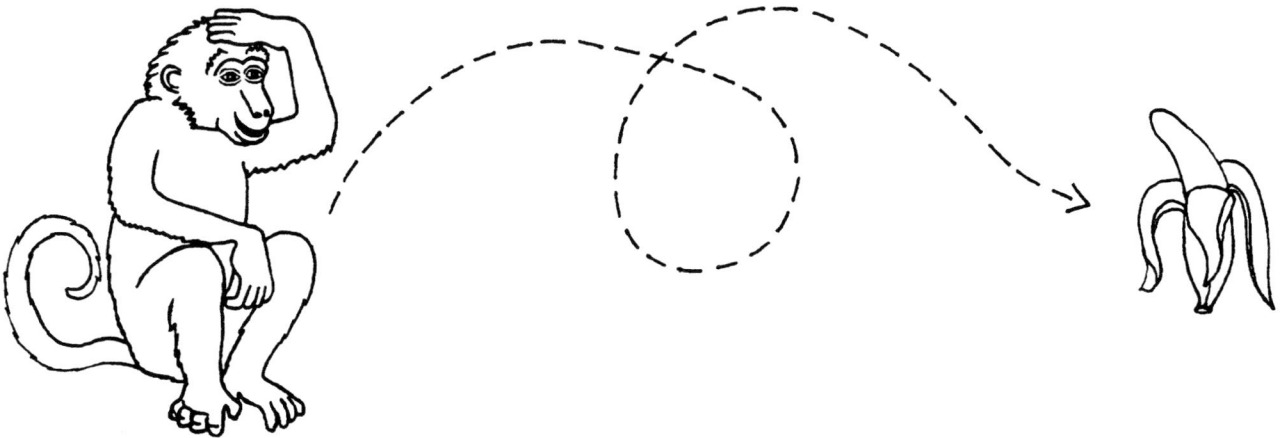

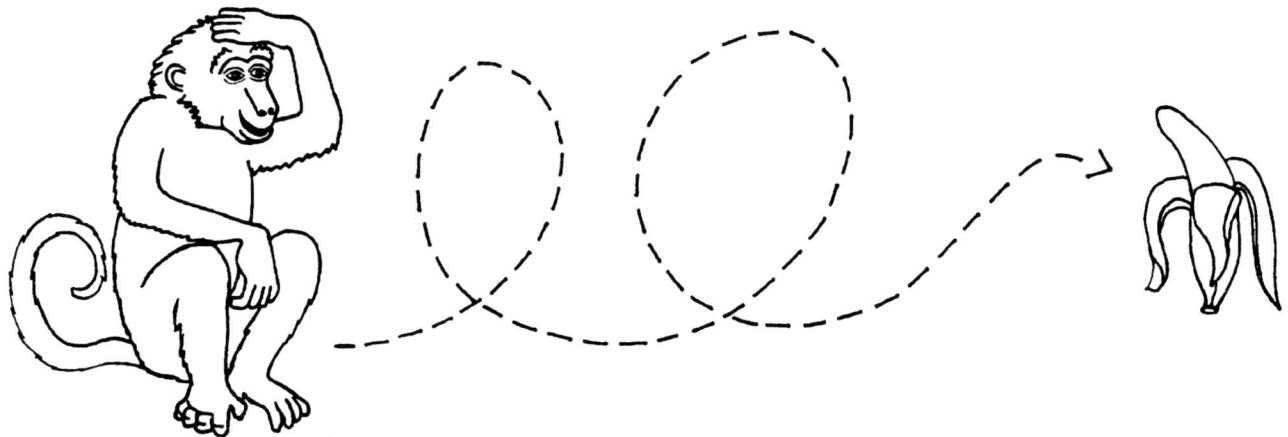

Activity 53: Squares Everywhere

Skill areas addressed

✔ in-hand manipulation, visual motor skills, scissors skills and grasp

Goal

✔ The child will cut out at least 3 squares with $1/4$" accuracy using correct scissors grasp.

Supplies Needed

Photocopies of the "Squares Everywhere" worksheet

Child safety scissors

Washable, nontoxic markers or crayons (optional)

Glue (optional)

Construction paper (optional)

Instructions

Instruct the child to cut out all 4 of the squares. Encourage the child to work slowly and stay on the black lines. If desired, the child could color in the squares with markers or crayons prior to cutting them out. (The child should attempt to color inside the square, but should not be expected to color inside the animals accurately.) Then the squares could be glued onto another sheet of paper in any design the child chooses.

Suggested Modifications and Adaptations

- Demonstrate the activity.
- If the child is having difficulty, provide assistance with holding and turning the paper as the child cuts the first square. However, the child's independence with manipulating the paper and cutting should improve as the activity continues.
- Provide physical assistance to change finger placement if the child grasps the scissors incorrectly. The child should maintain the wrist in a "thumb up" position while cutting.
- Consult the OT if the child is having significant difficulty cutting with accuracy or manipulating the paper for cutting.

Activity 53: Squares Everywhere (cont.)

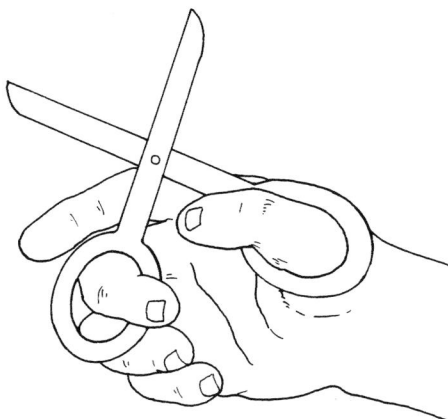

Correct, "thumb up" grasp

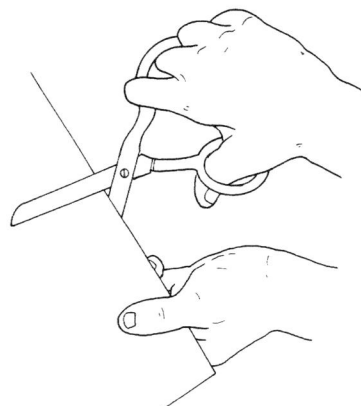

Immature, pronated grasp

Optional Fine Motor or Educational Extension Activities

- Have the child color 12 squares, 2 in each of 6 different colors. Then have the child cut out the squares and use them in a matching or memory game. (You can use copies of the worksheet for Activity 42: "X Marks the Spot" as templates for the squares.)
- Draw some additional squares or rectangles (or have the child draw them) on different-colored sheets of construction paper. Make sure the shapes are at least 2" on each side. Then have the child cut out the shapes and glue them onto another sheet to make a collage.
- Go on a treasure hunt around the room to find things that are square, or see who can name the most square things.

Squares Everywhere

Activity 54: Hopping down the Bunny Trail

Skill areas addressed

✔ visual motor skills, prewriting skills, pencil grasp, in-hand manipulation, coloring

Goal

✔ The child will independently trace the dotted lines with fair accuracy (the child's line stays within $3/8$" of the dotted lines). The child will color in the squares without coloring more than $3/8$" outside the lines.

Supplies Needed

Photocopies of the "Hopping down the Bunny Trail" worksheet

Washable, nontoxic markers

Instructions

First have the child trace the dotted lines of the squares with a marker. Next the child colors in the squares the bunny hops on. The child should not be expected to color the carrots or the rabbit accurately, only to color inside the squares. Finally, instruct the child to trace with a marker the dotted line of the trail that the bunny hops on to get the carrots. Encourage the child to work slowly in order to trace and color with accuracy.

Suggested Modifications and Adaptations

- Model the activity if the child has difficulty understanding the directions.
- Provide verbal cues and physical assistance as necessary.
- The child should be tracing with accuracy by this stage. If the child has difficulty tracing, consult the OT. Also consult the OT for techniques to facilitate a tripod grasp if the child continues to use an immature or palmar grasp on the marker.

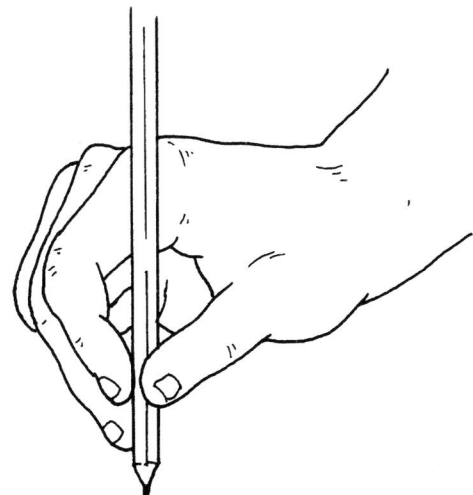

Dynamic tripod grasp

Activity 54: Hopping down the Bunny Trail (cont.)

Optional Fine Motor or Educational Extension Activities

- Discuss rabbits. What do they eat? Where do they live? Where might you see rabbits? What does their fur feel like?
- Bunnies hop. What other animals hop? What are other ways animals get around?
- Read children's stories about rabbits, such as *Peter Cottontail* or *The Velveteen Rabbit.*
- Have the child color in each square with a different marker, and name the color of each square.
- Have the child trace other dotted-line worksheets from preschool activity books. Choose fairly complex worksheets that have curved lines.
- Using a light-colored or highlighting marker, make some curved lines on a sheet of paper. Then have the child trace over your lines with a different marker to change the color of the lines. Encourage the child to try many markers to see all the different colors that result.
- Let the child draw some curved lines with a light-colored marker, then trace over them with a different color.

Hopping down the Bunny Trail

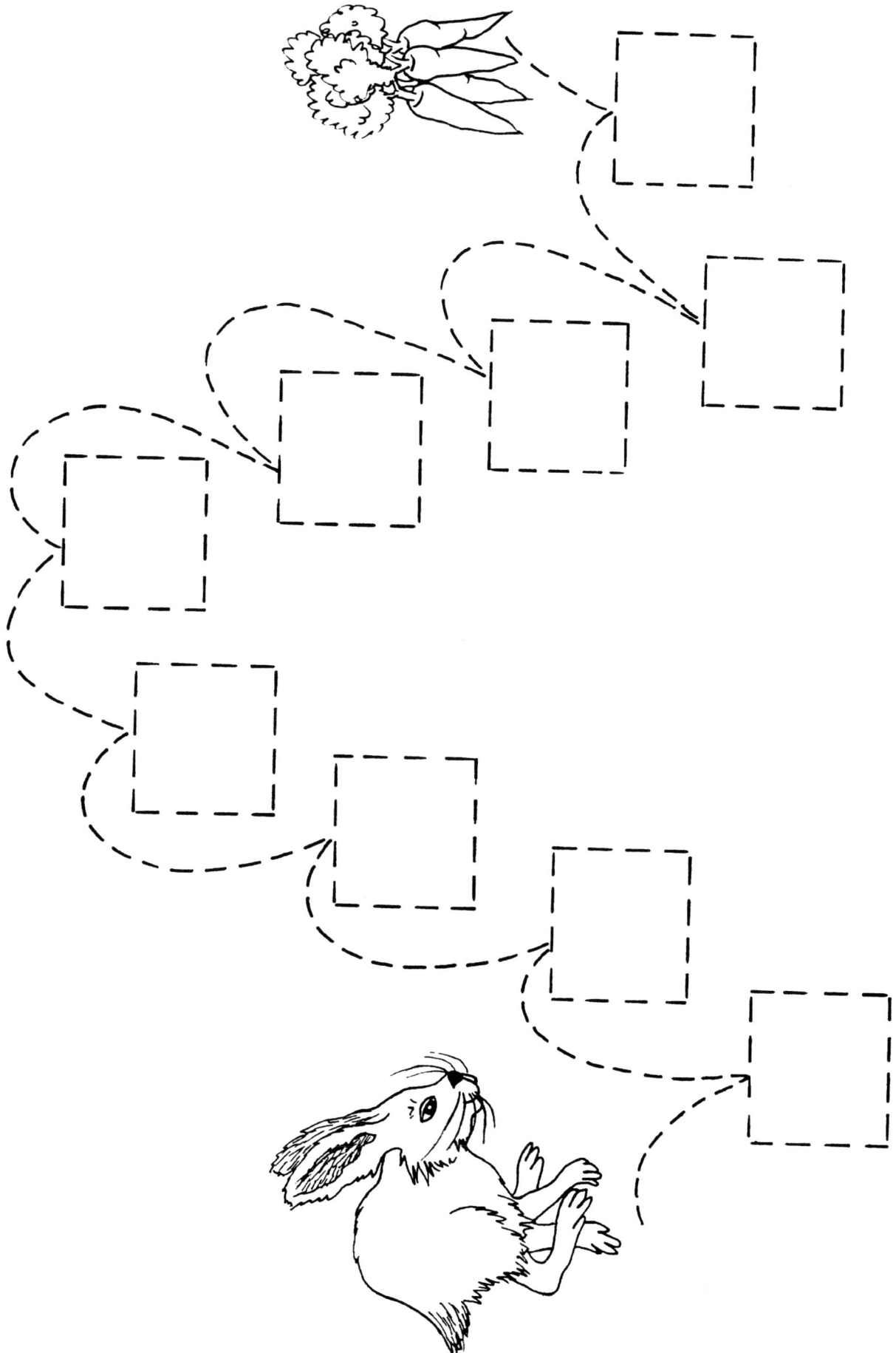

Activity 55: Copying Designs

Skill areas addressed

✔ visual motor skills, prewriting skills, pencil grasp, in-hand manipulation

Goal

✔ The child will draw the correct lines inside the shapes in the right column to make them match the models on the left.

Supplies Needed

Photocopies of the "Copying Designs" worksheet

Washable, nontoxic markers

Instructions

Instruct the child to draw lines in the second shape (right column) to make it look exactly like the first one (left column).

Suggested Modifications and Adaptations

- If the child has difficulty understanding the directions, demonstrate how to complete the activity.
- It may be helpful to put a blank piece of paper over the worksheet and uncover one pair of shapes at a time, to focus the child's attention.
- Make a second copy of the worksheet. Make an X inside the square, describing the lines as you draw them. Then have the child imitate this on his or her worksheet. Continue in this manner for each design on the page.
- Provide verbal cues and physical assistance as necessary.
- Consult the OT for techniques to facilitate a tripod grasp if the child continues to use an immature or palmar grasp on the marker. Also consult the OT if the child experiences significant difficulty or frustration with the activity.

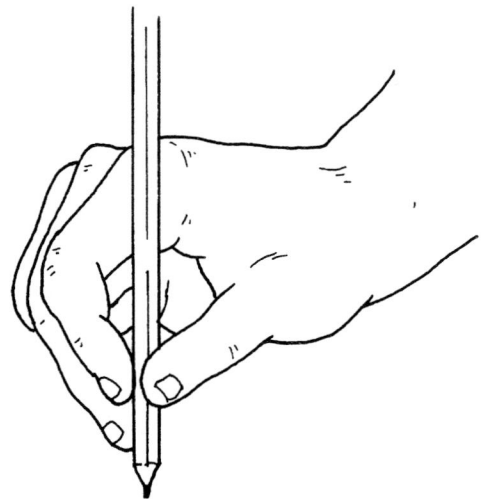

Dynamic tripod grasp

Activity 55: Copying Designs (cont.)

Optional Fine Motor or Educational Extension Activities

- Have the child label each of the shapes as he or she completes the objects.
- Draw other simple shapes or designs and have the child imitate them. Vary the materials and supplies used:

  Paints and an easel (standing)

  Chalk and chalkboard (standing)

  Paper and crayons on a large paper taped to the wall (standing)

  Shaving cream or talcum powder on a tabletop (sitting or standing)

Copying Designs

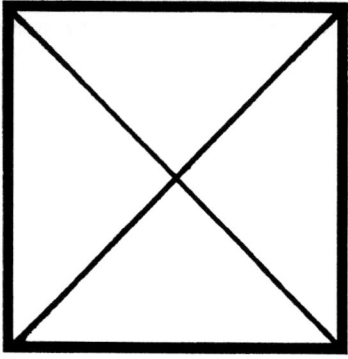

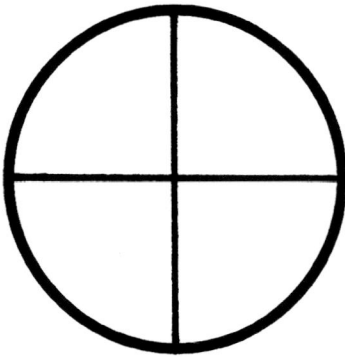

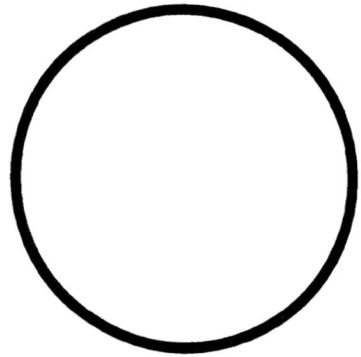

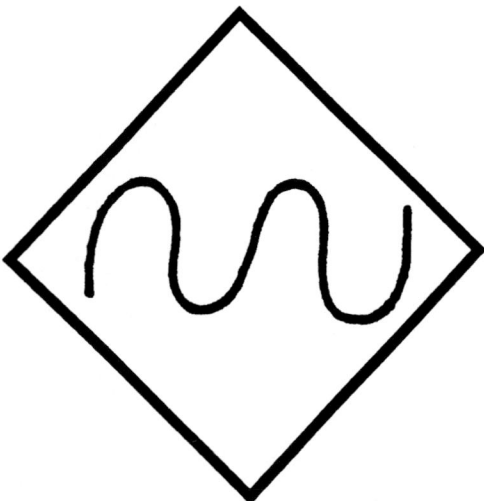

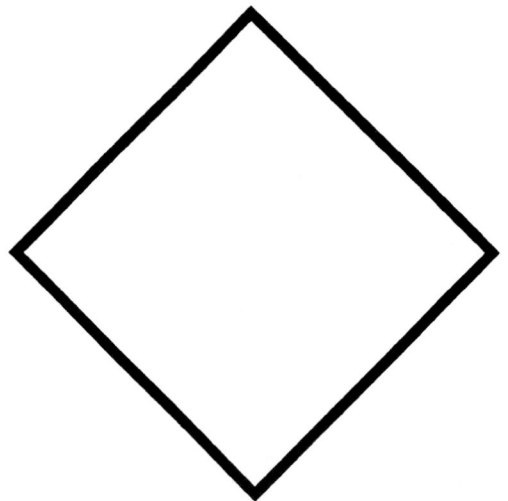

Activity 56: Making Small X's

Skill areas addressed

✔ in-hand manipulation, visual motor skills, prewriting skills, pencil grasp

Goal

✔ The child will make at least 12 X's by drawing diagonal lines from corner to corner within the squares.

Supplies Needed

At least 3 photocopies of the "Small X's" worksheet

Washable, nontoxic markers

Instructions

Instruct the child to make an X within each square. Verbally cue the child to make a diagonal line from the top left to lower right corners, then from top right to lower left. Encourage the child to go slowly and make straight diagonal lines from each corner.

Suggested Modifications and Adaptations

- Demonstrate the activity, verbally emphasizing going exactly from one top corner to the opposite bottom corner.
- If the child is having difficulty making diagonals, provide hand-over-hand assistance.
- Consult the OT if the child is having significant difficulty making straight diagonal lines (i.e., if the lines are more curved than diagonal).

Optional Fine Motor or Educational Extension Activities

- Draw some X's on a blank sheet of paper or on a chalkboard, then have the child attempt to copy them. If the child is unable to copy them independently, place dots at the beginning and ending points for each diagonal line.
- Draw shapes (triangle, diamond) and letters (N, M, W) that have diagonal lines in tactile materials (e.g., talcum powder, shaving cream, fingerpaint), and have the child trace over them.

Making Small X's

Activity 57: Imitating Squares

Skill areas addressed

✔ in-hand manipulation, visual motor skills, prewriting skills, pencil grasp

Goal

✔ The child will independently make 2 squares that have at least 3 good corners.

Supplies Needed

Large chalkboard (If a chalkboard is unavailable, use markers and butcher paper taped to a wall.)

Chalk

Instructions

Demonstrate drawing a square on the chalkboard. Emphasize making straight lines and turning the corners. Next, instruct the child to draw a square on the chalkboard, copying your model. Continue the activity until the child becomes proficient at making squares with at least 3 good corners.

Suggested Modifications and Adaptations

- Demonstrate the activity again, verbally emphasizing making straight lines and corners.
- Make a dot at each corner of the square to cue the child.
- If the child is having difficulty, provide hand-over-hand assistance, then fade to verbal cues as the child gains independence.
- Consult the OT for techniques to facilitate a tripod grasp if the child continues to use an immature or palmar grasp on the chalk. Also consult the OT if the child experiences significant difficulty or frustration with the activity.

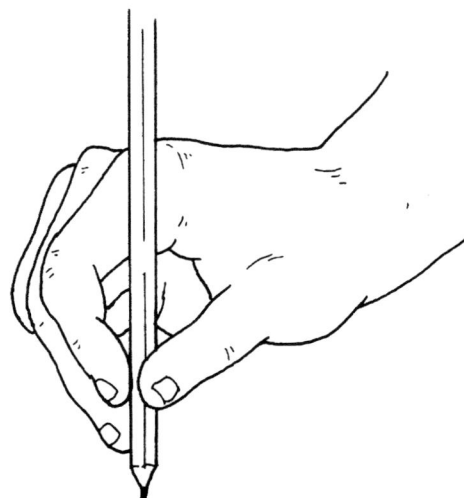

Dynamic tripod grasp

Activity 57: Imitating Squares (cont.)

Optional Fine Motor or Educational Extension Activities

- Repeat the same activity in a variety of media:
  Paints and an easel (standing)
  Paper and markers (sitting at a table)
  Crayons on a large sheet of paper taped to the wall (standing)
- Discuss the features of the squares the child drew (e.g., which are bigger or smaller than others, what colors they are, how many corners they have, etc.).
- In shaving cream or talcum powder on a tabletop, draw other shapes or letters with corners (e.g., triangle, rectangle, L, E, F). After drawing each shape or letter, have the child attempt to imitate it.

Activity 58: Master Builder

Skill areas addressed

✔ in-hand manipulation, visual motor skills

Goal

✔ The child will screw at least 5 screws into predrilled holes in wood.

Supplies Needed

10-12 medium-sized wood screws

Screwdriver (small enough for the child to handle easily)

Block of soft to semi-hard wood at least 5" x 5"

Drill

Instructions

In advance: Drill at least 12 holes, the size of the screws, into the piece of wood. You can use a random pattern or make letters, numbers or shapes. Make sure you can easily screw the screws into the holes.

With the child: Describe how to manipulate the screwdriver to drive a screw into one of the holes. Have the child screw in 5 screws at least halfway. If necessary, hold the block of wood steady to keep it from turning. The child may use a 2-handed grasp on the screwdriver if one hand is not strong enough.

Suggested Modifications and Adaptations

- Demonstrate screwing one of the screws into a hole.
- If the child is having difficulty, provide hand-over-hand assistance, then fade to verbal cues as the child gains independence.
- If the child is having difficulty starting the screw in the hole, provide physical assistance for the first few turns.
- Consult the OT if the child is unable to manipulate the screwdriver.

Activity 58: Master Builder (cont.)

Optional Fine Motor or Educational Extension Activities

- Drill holes to make the first letter of the child's name.
- After the screws are in place, the child could wind yarn around the screws to make different shapes. With 2 identical sets of screws, you could make a yarn design and have the child try to imitate it.
- Vary the type and size of screws used.
- Vary the material the screws go into (e.g., different types of wood, foam plastic).

Activity 59: Family Portrait

Skill areas addressed

✔ visual motor skills, prewriting skills, pencil grasp

Goal

✔ The child will draw people with at least 5 recognizable body parts.

Supplies Needed

White construction paper

Black permanent marker or crayon

Watercolors and paintbrushes

Small glass of water

Painting smock or painting shirt to protect the child's clothing

Activity 59: Family Portrait (cont.)

Instructions

Begin by discussing what a family is and the members of the child's family. Instruct the child to draw a picture of his or her family with the black marker or crayon. If the people the child is drawing are unrecognizable, encourage the child to try again. Then allow the child to color in the family using the watercolors. (The focus of the activity is drawing people, so if the child chooses to draw an imaginary family, that is fine.)

Suggested Modifications and Adaptations

- Demonstrate the activity. Have the child watch you draw your family on a piece of paper. While you are drawing, name each person and describe the different body parts you are drawing (eyes, nose, mouth, hair, arms, legs, hands, feet, etc.).
- Draw one person at a time. As the child watches, name the body parts you are drawing and what shapes you are using to make each one. Then have the child draw himself or herself. Repeat in this fashion for each member of the family.
- Provide verbal instructions and physical cues for using the watercolors as necessary.

Optional Fine Motor or Educational Extension Activities

- Incorporate the activity into a discussion or a unit on different kinds of families. In a class or group, you can have all children complete this activity. Then have a "show and tell" time where the children can show their portraits and talk about their family.
- Draw a family using different media:
    Paint at an easel (standing)
    Shaving cream on a tabletop (sitting)
    Markers on paper at a table (sitting) or on the wall (standing)
    Frosting or ketchup on a flat, washable surface (sitting)
- Have the child attempt to draw other easy representative figure (house, tree, sun, flower, etc.). Talk about the different shapes used to make each figure.

Activity 60: Triangles and Diamonds

Skill areas addressed

✔ in-hand manipulation, visual motor skills, prewriting skills, pencil grasp

Goal

✔ The child will draw straight lines connecting the dots in numerical order to make squares and diamonds.

Supplies Needed

Photocopies of the "Triangles and Diamonds" worksheet

Washable, nontoxic markers or crayons

Instructions

Instruct the child to connect the dots of each of the 4 pictures, beginning at dot #1 and connecting the dots in numerical order. Encourage the child to make straight lines between the dots.

Suggested Modifications and Adaptations

- Demonstrate how to connect the dots if the child is having difficulty understanding the directions.
- If the child has difficulty concentrating on one picture at a time, you can cover all but one picture with blank paper.
- If the child is having difficulty connecting the dots, provide hand-over-hand assistance, then fade to verbal cues as the child gains independence. By the end of this activity, the child should be making straight lines to form shapes independently.
- Consult the OT for techniques to facilitate a tripod grasp if the child continues to use an immature or palmar grasp on the markers. Also consult the OT if the child experiences significant difficulty or frustration with the activity.
- Provide assistance to recognize each number in numerical order as necessary.

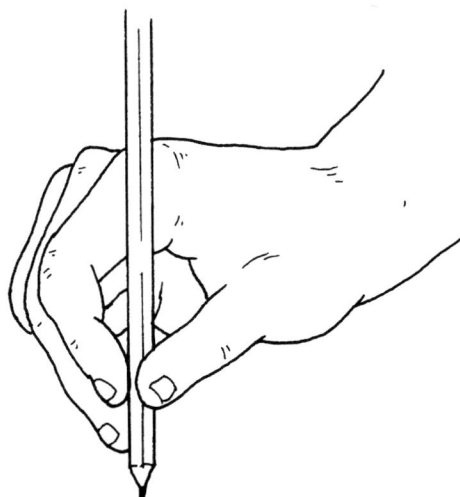

Dynamic tripod grasp

Activity 60: Triangles and Diamonds (cont.)

Optional Fine Motor or Educational Extension Activities

- Have the child identify each shape once the dots are connected. Then have the child color the matching shapes the same color.
- Make up easy connect-the-dots activities (with 4-5 dots each) for the child to practice with.

Triangles and Diamonds

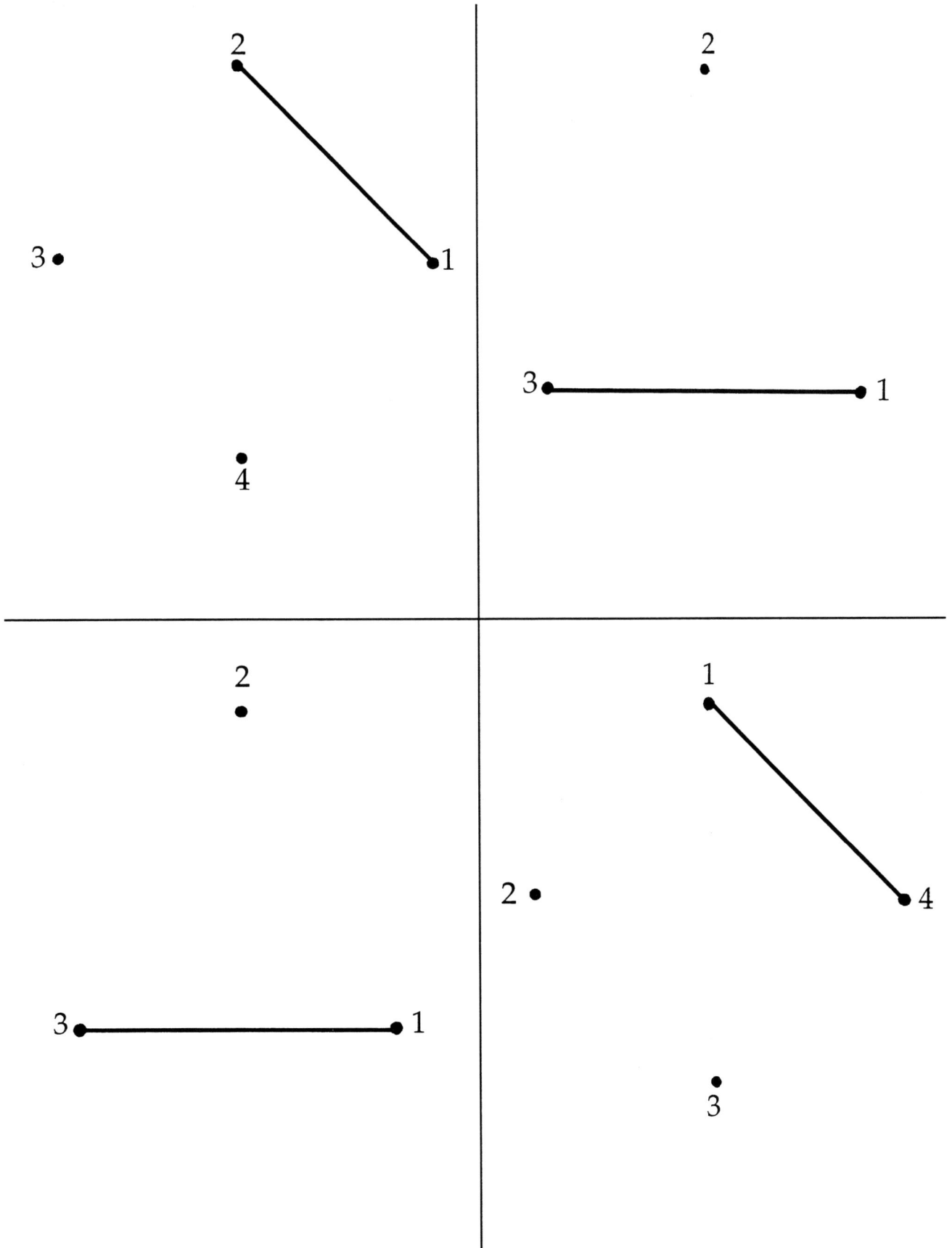

Activity 61: Spiral

Skill areas addressed

✔ in-hand manipulation, visual motor skills, scissors skills and grasp

Goal

✔ The child will cut out the spiral with $3/8$" accuracy, using correct scissors grasp.

Supplies Needed

Photocopies of the "Spiral" worksheet

Photocopies of the "Jumping Kangaroo" worksheet (optional)

Child safety scissors

Washable, nontoxic markers (optional)

Hole punch and string (optional)

Instructions

Extend the spiral to the edge of the worksheet using a black marker to direct the child where to start cutting. Instruct the child to cut out the entire spiral by cutting on the black line only. Make sure the child does not snip across the strips and cut the spiral in two. The child should maintain the wrist in a "thumb up" position while cutting. For fun, after cutting out the spiral, the child may hold it by one end and bounce it up and down, pretending it is a snake. (Draw eyes, spots, etc., on the snake, if desired.)

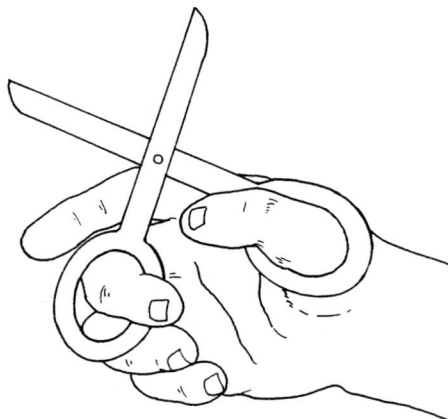

Correct, "thumb up" grasp   Immature, pronated grasp

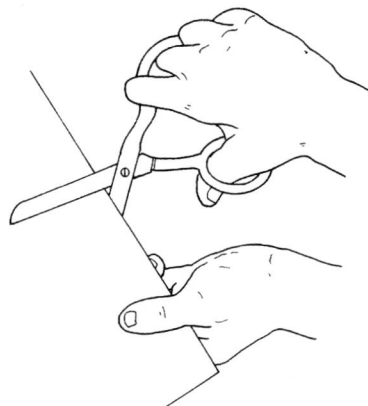

Activity 61: Spiral (cont.)

The activity can be expanded by having the child cut out the kangaroo on page 175 and glue it on the end of the spiral. (Provide assistance as necessary to cut out the animal.) When the glue dries, the child can make the animal jump around. If desired, punch a hole in the end of the spiral and hang the jumping kangaroo from the ceiling with string.

Suggested Modifications and Adaptations

- Demonstrate the activity if the child is having difficulty understanding the directions.
- Provide verbal cues throughout the activity as necessary.
- Provide initial hand-over-hand assistance with turning and manipulating the paper while cutting to allow the child to feel the required motions.

Optional Fine Motor or Educational Extension Activities

- See how many animals the child can name that hop. (Rabbits, kangaroos, grasshoppers, frogs, toads, etc.)
- Draw curvy snakes on a large piece of construction paper, then have the child cut them out.
- The child may cut out other simple pictures of single objects (ball, kite, dog, cat, etc.); look in preschool activity and coloring books for appropriate pictures. Select something that has a clear outline and does not have many short or angular cuts.

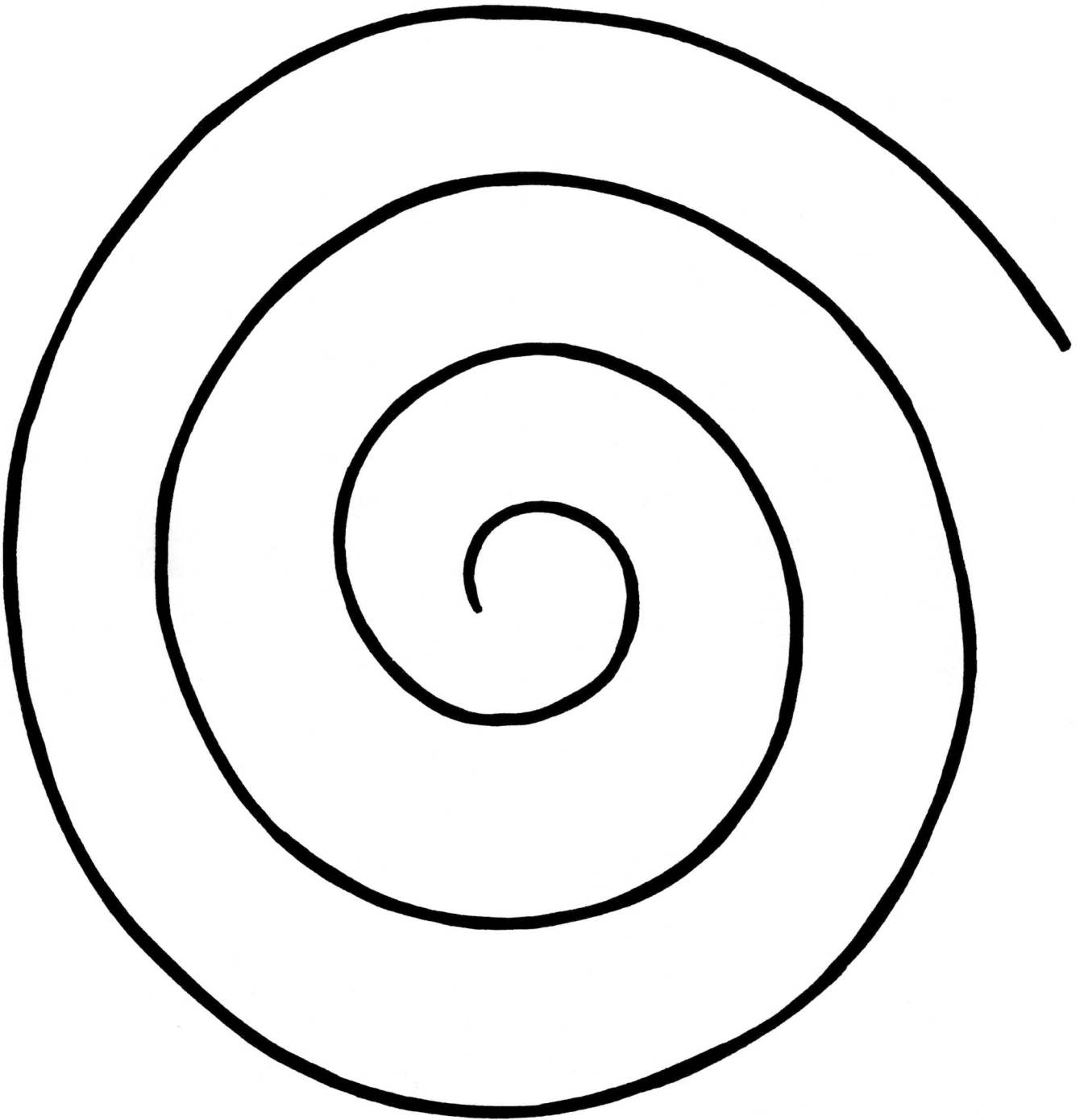

Spiral

Jumping Kangaroo

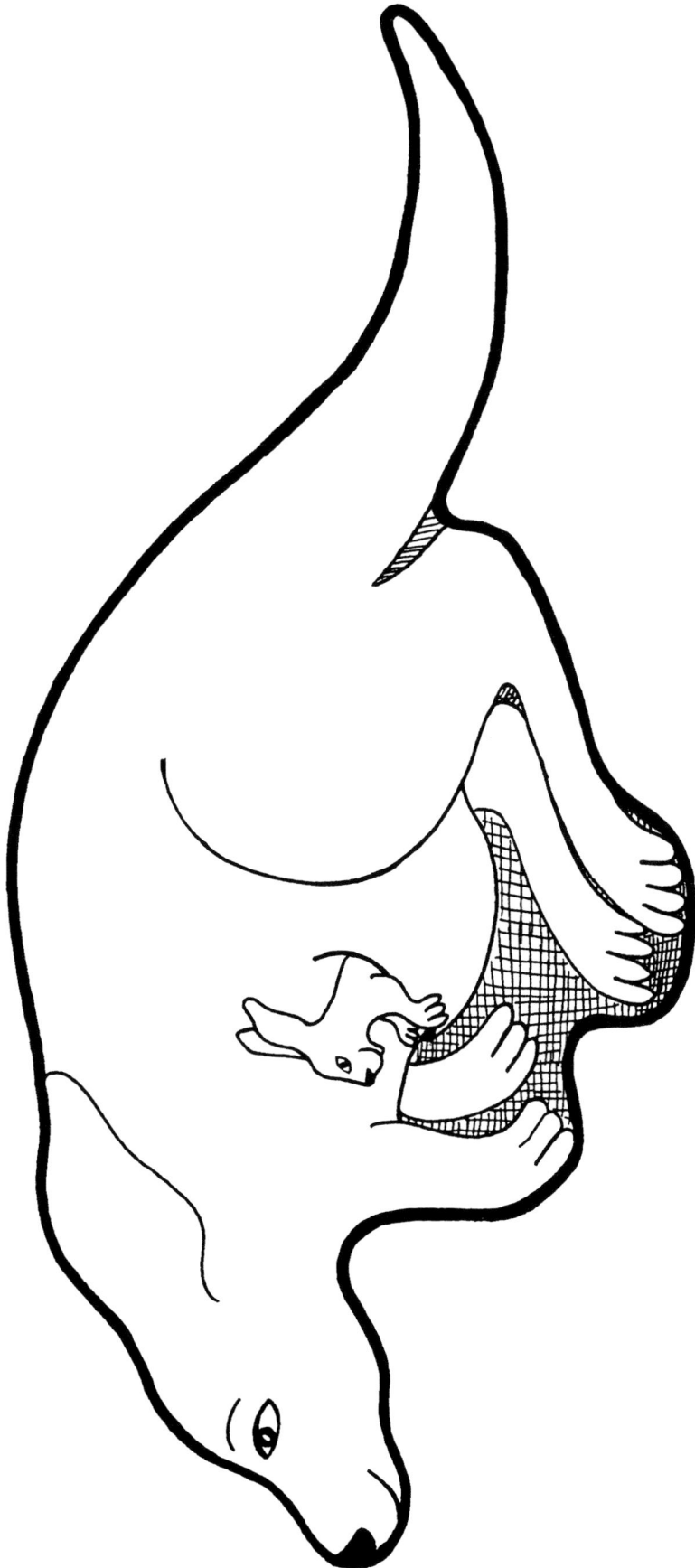

Activity 62: Paper Bag Face Puppets

Skill areas addressed

✔ visual motor skills, scissors skills and grasp, pencil grasp, in-hand manipulation

Goal

✔ The child will cut out the puppet's facial features with sufficient accuracy to make a recognizable puppet and will use correct scissors grasp.

Supplies Needed

Small paper lunch bag

Construction paper (Allow the child to choose the colors.)

Child safety scissors

Washable, nontoxic markers

Glue

Instructions

First allow the child to choose a color or colors of construction paper for the puppet's eyes, nose and mouth. Then draw a large semicircle for a mouth, a smaller semicircle for the nose and circles for the eyes. Instruct the child to cut out the mouth, nose and eyes and glue them onto the paper bag. The mouth should go with the flat edge flush against the fold of the bottom of the bag. The eyes and nose go on the bottom of the bag. Finally instruct the child to use markers to add facial features such as eyeballs, eyebrows, teeth and hair.

Activity 62: Paper Bag Face Puppets (cont.)

Suggested Modifications and Adaptations

- Demonstrate making a paper bag face if the child is having difficulty understanding the directions.
- Model the activity step-by-step, having the child imitate each step immediately after you complete it.
- Consult the OT if the child has significant difficulty with the task or needs assistance with scissors grasp and cutting with accuracy.

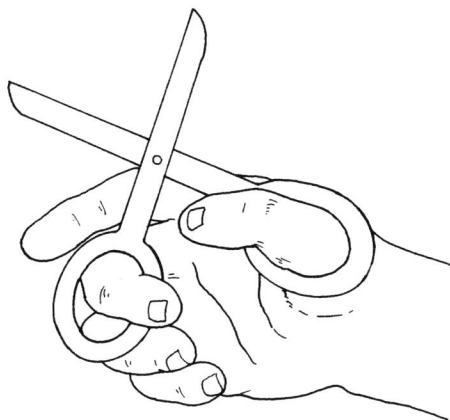

Correct, "thumb up" grasp   Immature, pronated grasp

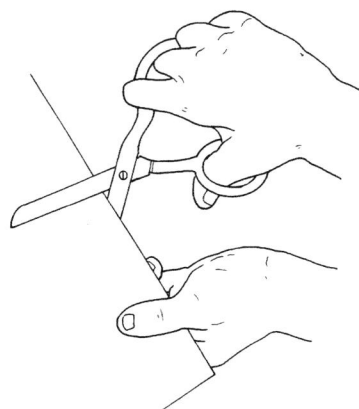

Optional Fine Motor or Educational Extension Activities

- Have the child draw and cut out additional features such as ears and a hat from construction paper. Then these items can be glued on the paper bag face puppet.
- Encourage the child to use the puppet in dramatic play or to make up a puppet show.

Activity 63: Beautiful Bugs, Part 1

Skill areas addressed

✔ in-hand manipulation, visual motor skills, scissors skills and grasp

Goal

✔ The child will cut out the parts of the insect with $1/4$" accuracy, using correct scissor grasp and manipulating the paper independently.

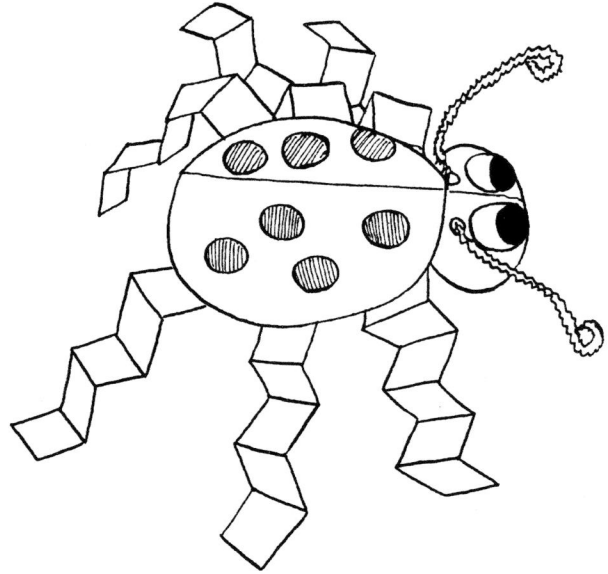

Supplies Needed

2-4 sheets of construction paper
(Allow the child to choose the color or colors.)

Child safety scissors

Black marker

Instructions

Begin this activity with a discussion of what kind of bug the child would like to make (for example, a spider, grasshopper, centipede, ladybug, ant, etc.). Then determine what body shape and color this animal should have and how many legs it has. Depending on the type of bug, the child may choose to make the head and body as one piece or to make 2 separate pieces. Next allow the child to choose colors for the body and legs (and head, if desired). Draw 2 identical body shapes (approximately 4" across) on the construction paper for the body, 2 identical shapes about 2" across for the head (if desired), and 8" lines approximately $3/4$" apart on a piece of construction paper for the legs (6 lines for an insect, 8 for a spider or scorpion).

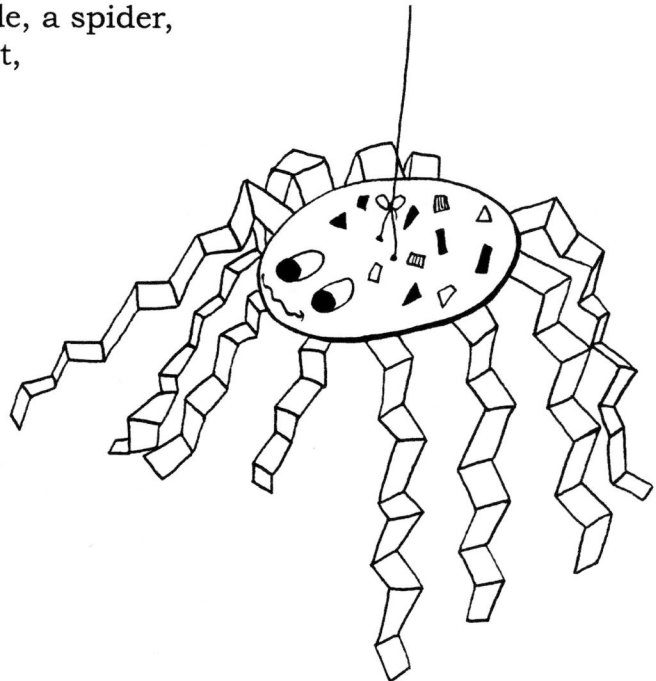

Activity 63: Beautiful Bugs, Part 1 (cont.)

Instruct the child to cut the strips apart and cut out the 2 body shapes (and 2 head shapes if desired). If the child has good attention to task and wants to finish the insect, proceed to Activity 64. Otherwise, set aside all the strips and body parts until the child is ready for the next activity.

Suggested Modifications and Adaptations

- Demonstrate the activity by drawing and cutting out your own insect.
- If the child has difficulty manipulating the paper while cutting, provide initial hand-over-hand assistance, then fade to verbal cues as the child gains independence. The child should, however, be able to complete most of the activity without assistance.
- If the child is having serious difficulty maintaining a correct scissors grasp and cutting with accuracy, consult the OT. The child should maintain the wrist in "thumb up" position while cutting.

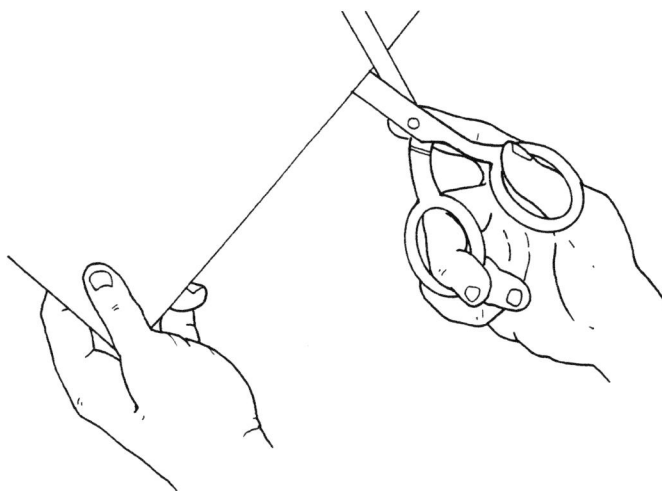

Holding scissors while manipulating paper

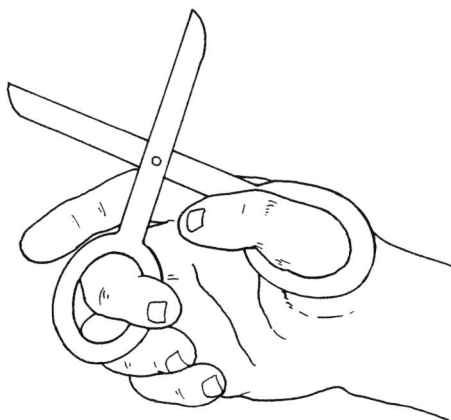

Correct, "thumb up" grasp

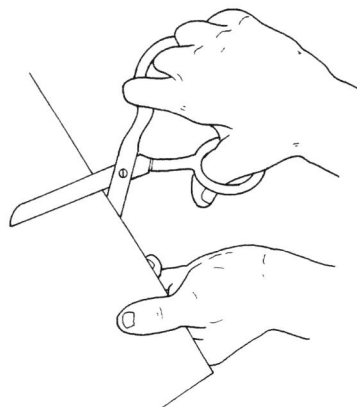

Immature, pronated grasp

Optional Fine Motor or Educational Extension Activities

- Help the child learn some basic information about the insect or arachnid he or she has chosen to make. How does it move? Does it live in groups or alone? What does it eat? Is it harmful or helpful to people?

Activity 64: Beautiful Bugs, Part 2

Skill areas addressed

✔ in-hand manipulation, visual motor skills

Goal

✔ The child will independently accordion fold each strip of paper at least 6 times.

Supplies Needed

Insect body parts from the previous activity

Washable, nontoxic markers

Small scraps of construction paper

Glue

Long piece of string (optional)

Hole punch (optional)

Pipe cleaners (optional)

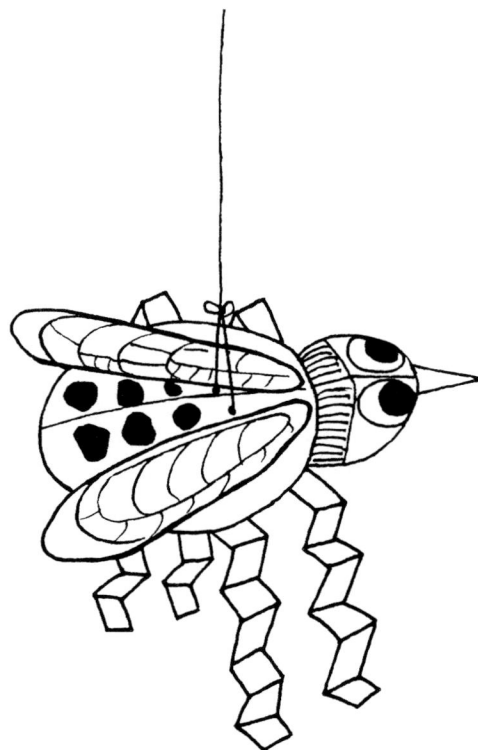

Instructions

Instruct the child to accordion fold the paper strips for insect legs. Next, have the child glue the identical body parts together, matching up the edges, to strengthen the paper. Let the child assemble the head and body, if separate, then glue the legs around the edges of the body. The child can put eyes on the insect using the scraps of construction paper or by drawing them on with markers. Depending on the child's abilities, pipe cleaner antennae, wings, or other features may also be added. Finally, if the child wants to hang up the insect, punch 2 holes in the center of the body. Then have the child lace the string through the holes and assist with knotting the string.

Activity 64: Beautiful Bugs, Part 2 (cont.)

Suggested Modifications and Adaptations

- Demonstrate the activity by assembling your own insect.
- If the child has difficulty with accordion folding, provide hand-over-hand assistance initially, then fade to verbal instructions as the child gains independence.

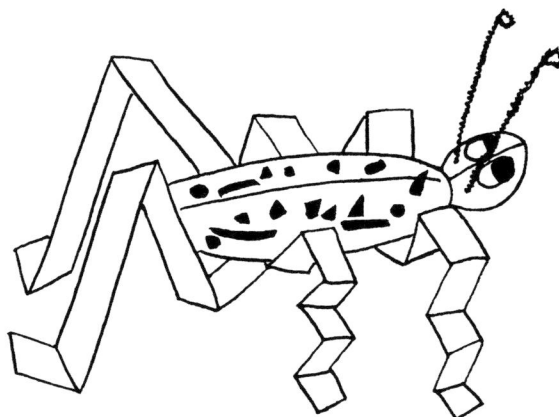

Optional Fine Motor or Educational Extension Activities

- The child can make a paper chain by cutting (and, if desired, accordion folding) 2" strips of paper. Then demonstrate how to glue together interlocking circles to form a chain.

Activity 65: Help the Raccoon Get Home

Skill areas addressed

✔ in-hand manipulation, visual motor skills, prewriting skills, pencil grasp

Goal

✔ The child will independently draw a line through the path without crossing the outer black lines more than once.

Supplies Needed

Photocopies of the "Help the Raccoon Get Home" worksheet

Washable, nontoxic markers

Instructions

Instruct the child to draw a line along the path to help the raccoon find the way back to its cave. Instruct the child to work slowly so as to stay within the black lines.

Suggested Modifications and Adaptations

- If the child has difficulty understanding the directions, complete a worksheet yourself to demonstrate the task.
- If this activity appears too difficult for the child, repeat Activity 37 ("Help the Spider Get to Its Web") and Activity 43 ("Help the Mouse Get the Cheese") to provide practice with simpler paths. Then reintroduce this worksheet.
- Consult the OT for techniques to facilitate a tripod grasp if the child continues to use an immature or palmar grasp on the marker.

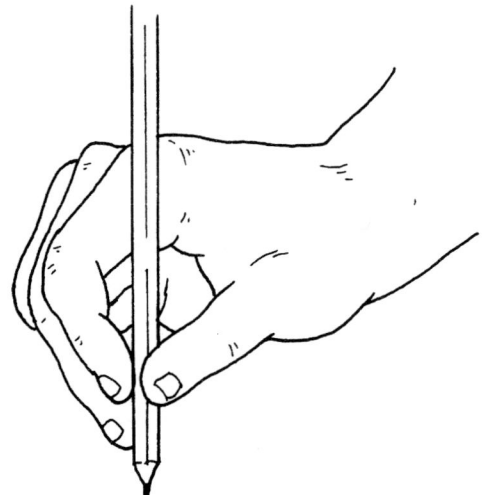

Dynamic tripod grasp

Activity 65: Help the Raccoon Get Home (cont.)

Optional Fine Motor or Educational Extension Activities

- Discuss raccoons and their habits. Where do they live? What do they eat? What special characteristics do they have?
- Introduce other pathway or maze worksheets that have paths with corners and diagonals. Make sure the path the child is to follow is quite obvious. Such worksheets can be found in many preschool activity books.
- Make up large pathways with diagonal lines and corners on butcher paper. Have the child draw a line through the path with a marker, then if desired, travel through it with a toy car or boat.

Help the Raccoon Get Home

Activity 66: Imitation X

Skill areas addressed

✔ in-hand manipulation, visual motor skills, prewriting skills, pencil grasp

Goal

✔ The child will imitate at least 3 X's, making good diagonal lines.

Supplies Needed

Washable, nontoxic markers

Large pieces of white construction paper

Instructions

Demonstrate drawing an X on the construction paper (with lines approximately 2" in length). Emphasize making straight diagonal lines in a downward direction. Instruct the child to draw an X on the construction paper. Have the child attempt to make at least 10 X's.

Suggested Modifications and Adaptations

- Continue to demonstrate making X's, describing the process each time.
- If the child is having difficulty with the activity, provide hand-over-hand assistance, then fade to verbal cues as the child gains independence.
- If necessary, draw dots at the beginning and ending points of both diagonal lines to assist the child in understanding where to draw the lines.
- Consult the OT for techniques to facilitate a tripod grasp if the child continues to use an immature or palmar grasp on the marker. Also consult the OT if the child experiences significant difficulty or frustration with the activity.

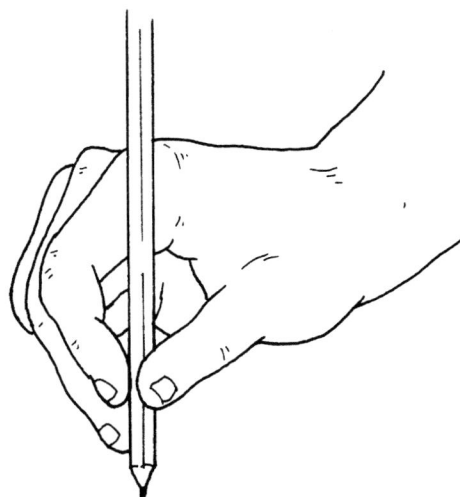

Dynamic tripod grasp

Activity 66: Imitation X (cont.)

Optional Fine Motor or Educational Extension Activities

- Draw other letters that have diagonal lines (W, Y, N, M, V, Z, K), and have the child attempt to imitate them.
- Repeat the same activity in a variety of media:
    Paints and an easel (standing)
    Chalk and a chalkboard (standing)
    Paper and crayons on a large sheet of paper taped to the wall (standing)
    Shaving cream or finger-paint (sitting at a table)
- Teach the child how to play "tic-tac-toe," having the child make the X's.

Activity 67: Home, Sweet Home

Skill areas addressed

✔ visual motor skills, scissors skills and grasp, pencil grasp, coloring, in-hand manipulation

Goal

✔ The child will color in at least 75% of each house without going more than $3/8$" beyond the outer border; the child will independently cut out the houses with $1/4$" accuracy.

Supplies Needed

Photocopies of the 2 "Home, Sweet Home" worksheets

Washable, nontoxic markers

Child safety scissors

Glue

Instructions

Instruct the child to color in the houses and roofs on worksheet 1, then to cut out the houses and roofs (4 items). Make sure the child maintains the wrist in a "thumb up" position while cutting, rather than turning the scissors sideways. Finally instruct the child to match up the correct houses and roofs with the outlines on worksheet 2. The child can glue the colored-in pieces on these outlines.

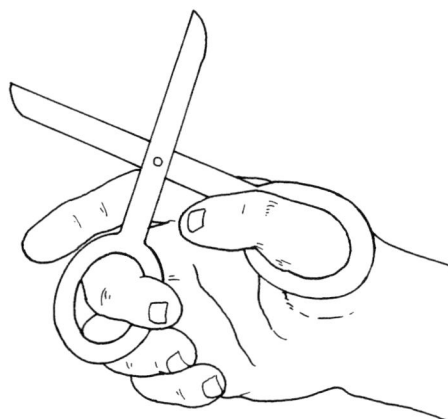

Correct, "thumb up" grasp   Immature, pronated grasp

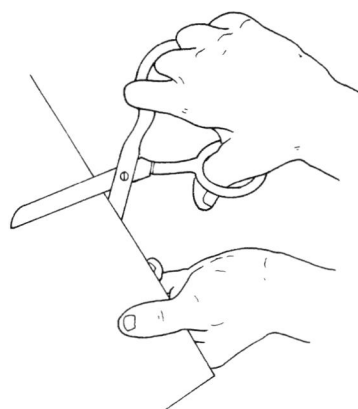

Activity 67: Home, Sweet Home (cont.)

Suggested Modifications and Adaptations

- Demonstrate the activity if the child has difficulty understanding the directions; if necessary, complete the activity step-by-step, having the child do each step immediately after you model it.
- Provide initial hand-over-hand assistance and verbal cues as necessary to assist the child to begin coloring and to manipulate the paper while cutting.
- Consult the OT for techniques to facilitate a tripod grasp if the child continues to use an immature or palmar grasp on the markers. Also consult the OT if the child experiences significant difficulty or frustration with the activity.

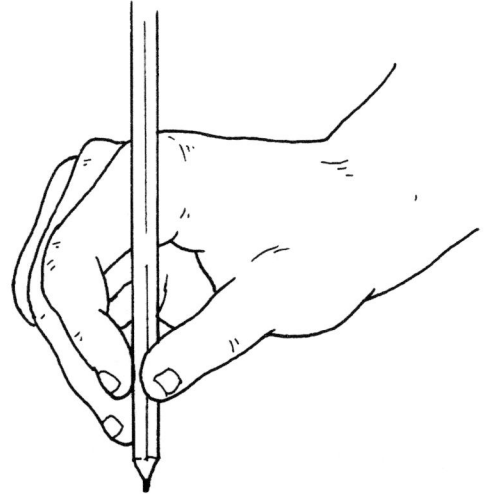

Optional Fine Motor or Educational Extension Activities

- Discuss different types of dwellings with the child. Does the child live in a house, an apartment or a townhome? What can houses be made of? What is the child's home made of? Why do people need homes? Look at pictures of the kinds of homes people in other cultures live in. How are these homes like and unlike the child's home?
- Look in preschool activity books for other color, cut out and paste activities.
- Have the child draw his or her own house. Label the parts of the house, including windows, front door, roof, etc.

Dynamic tripod grasp

Home, Sweet Home 1

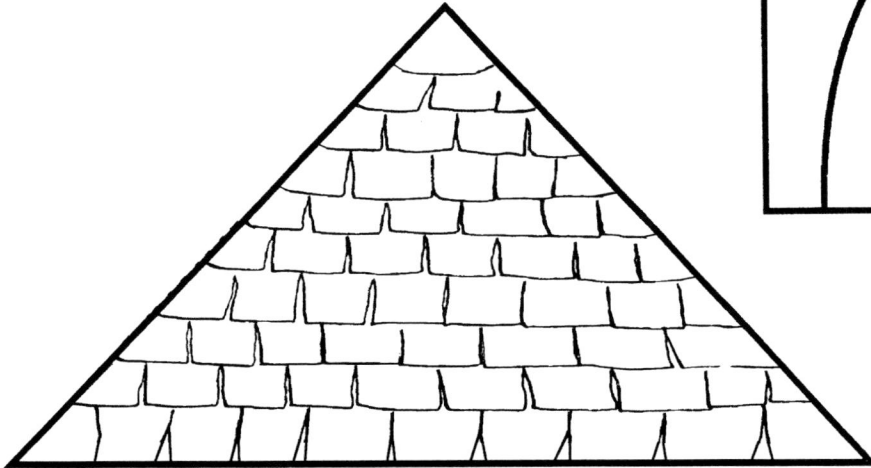

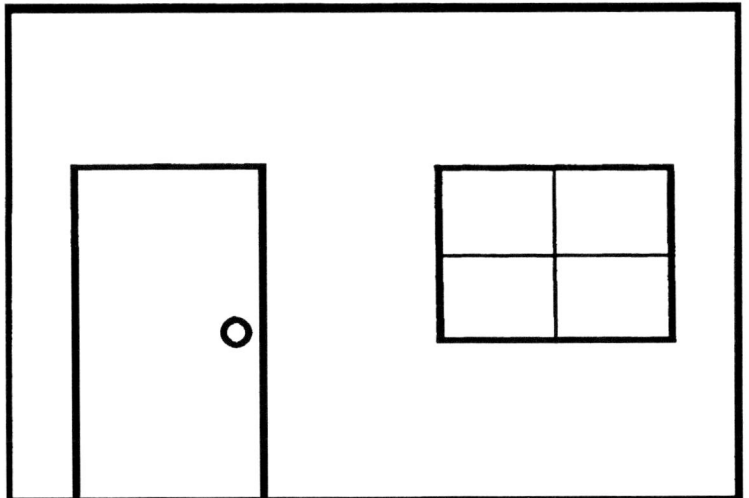

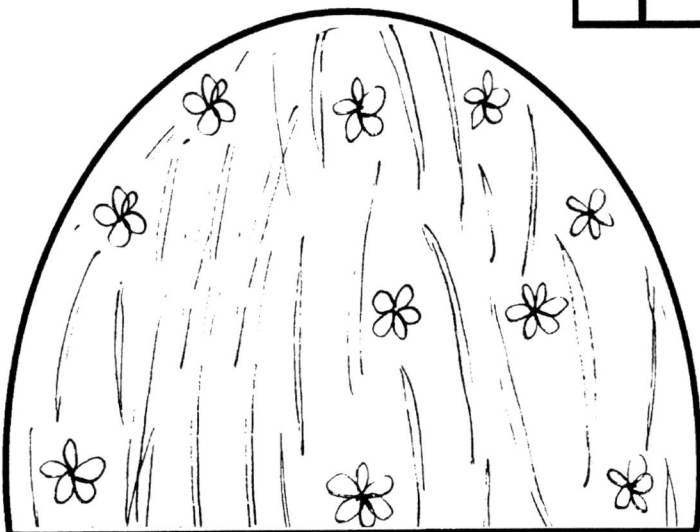

Home, Sweet Home 2

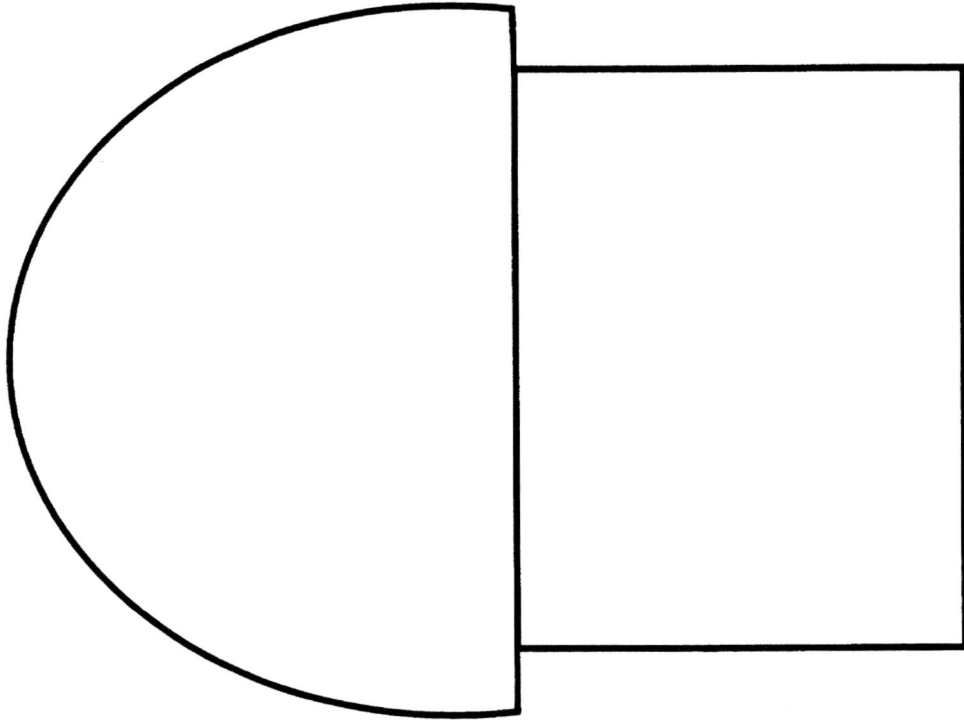

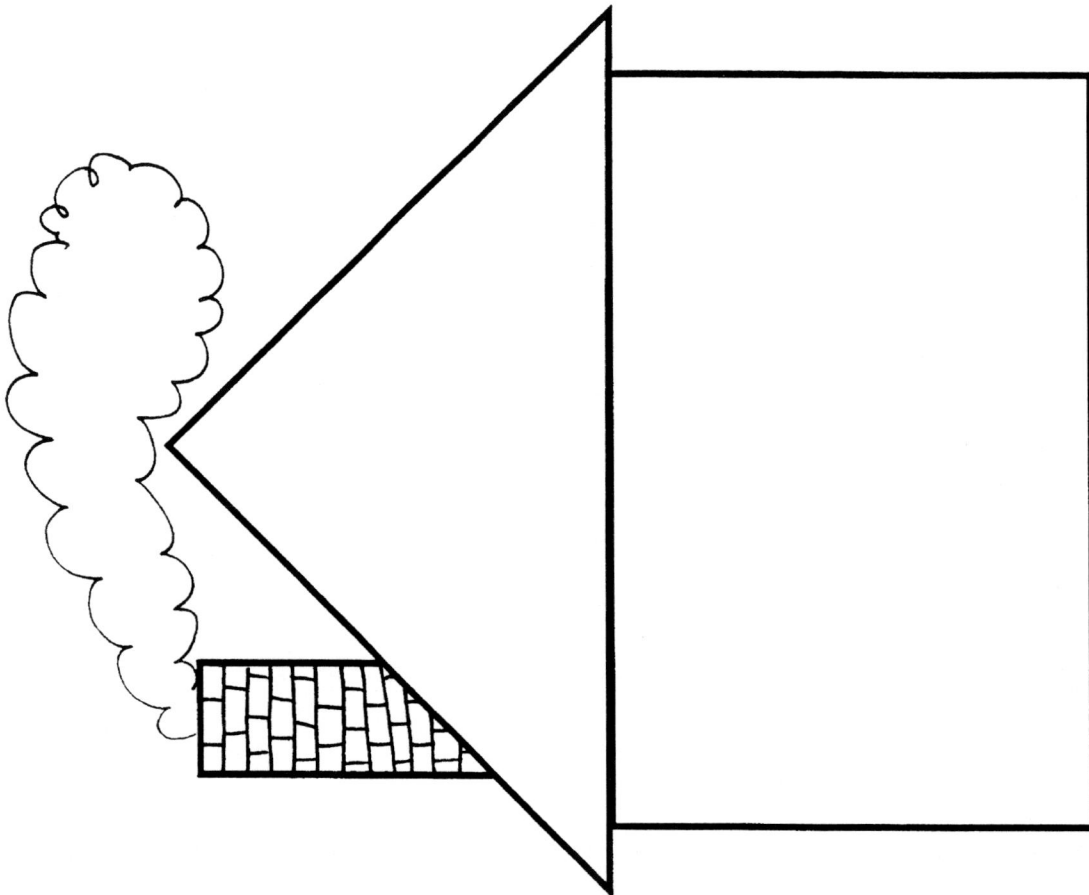

Activity 68: Connect the Dots

Skill areas addressed

✔ visual motor skills, in-hand manipulation, prewriting skills, pencil grasp

Goal

✔ The child will draw straight lines connecting the dots in numerical order to form the house.

Supplies Needed

Photocopies of the "Connect the Dots" worksheet

Washable, nontoxic markers

Instructions

Instruct the child to start with dot #1 and connect all the dots in numerical order to see what the picture is. Encourage the child to make straight lines between the dots.

Suggested Modifications and Adaptations

- Model the activity, demonstrating how to connect the dots, if the child has difficulty understanding the directions.
- Provide verbal and hand-over-hand assistance as necessary.
- Consult the OT for techniques to facilitate a tripod grasp if the child continues to use an immature or palmar grasp on the marker. Also consult the OT if the child experiences significant difficulty or frustration with the activity.
- Provide assistance to recognize the numbers in numerical order as necessary.

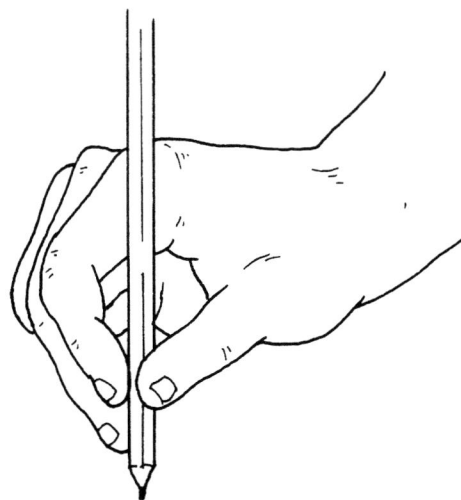

Dynamic tripod grasp

Activity 68: Connect the Dots (cont.)

Optional Fine Motor or Educational Extension Activities

- Have the child color in the house once all the dots are connected.
- Make up other easy dot-to-dot worksheets (with 10-15 dots).
- Look in preschool activity books to find other simple dot-to-dot activities. (Choose simple worksheets with no more than 20 dots.)
- Have the child attempt to draw his or her own house. Talk about the shapes used to draw a house (rectangle, squares, triangle, etc.). The child could add trees, flowers, sun, family members and so on to the representational drawing.

Connect the Dots

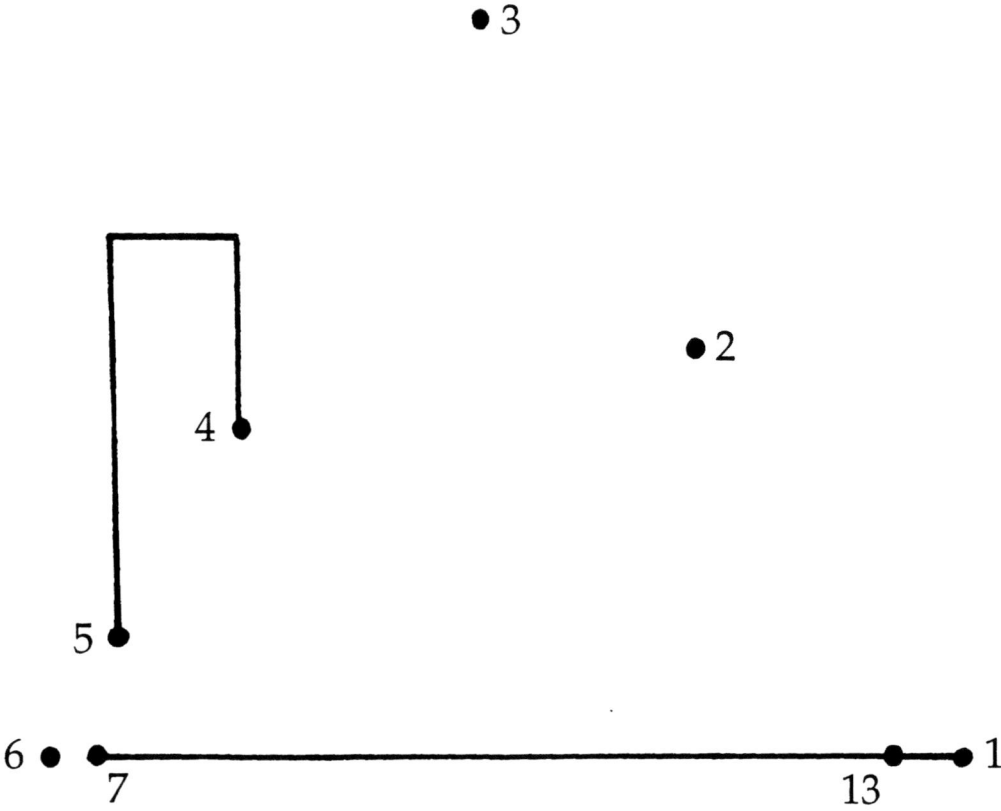

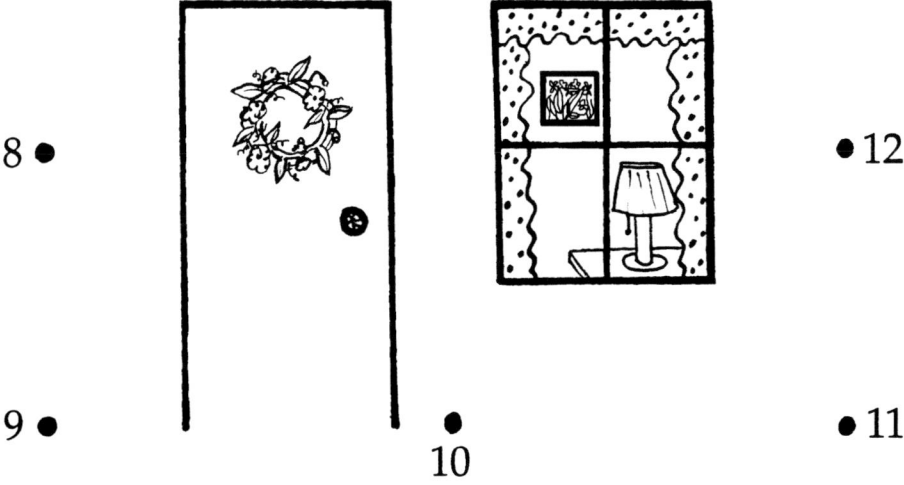

● 3

● 2

4 ●

5 ●

6 ● ● 1
7 ● 13 ●

8 ●

12 ●

9 ●

10 ●

11 ●

Activity 69: Can You Picture This?

Skill areas addressed

✔ visual motor skills, in-hand manipulation, prewriting skills, pencil grasp

Goal

✔ The child will complete the partial pictures in the right column by adding the correct lines to match the pictures in the left column.

Supplies Needed

Photocopies of the "Can You Picture This?" worksheet

Washable, nontoxic markers or crayons

Instructions

Instruct the child to complete each partial picture in the right column to make it look exactly like the picture in the left column.

Suggested Modifications and Adaptations

- If the child has difficulty understanding the directions, demonstrate how to complete the activity.
- Cover all but one pair of pictures with a blank sheet of paper to help focus the child's attention.
- Complete the activity one step at a time, describing how to complete the step as you do it. Have the child imitate each step immediately after you do it.
- Provide verbal cues and physical assistance as necessary.
- Consult the OT for techniques to facilitate a tripod grasp if the child continues to use an immature or palmar grasp on the marker. Also consult the OT if the child experiences significant difficulty or frustration completing the activity.

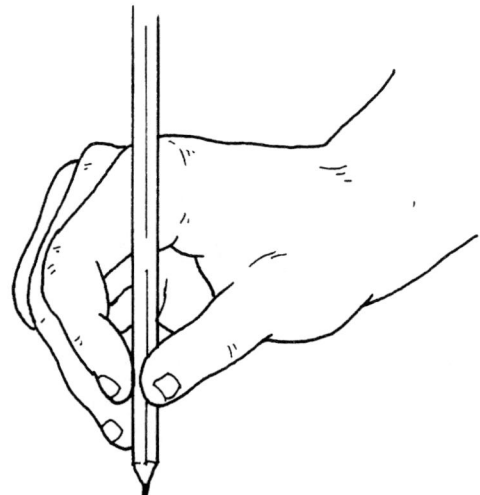

Dynamic tripod grasp

Activity 69: Can You Picture This? (cont.)

Optional Fine Motor or Educational Extension Activities

- Have the child label each of the objects as he or she completes it.
- Draw other simple pictures or designs and have the child imitate them.
  Use a variety of media:
  Paints and an easel (standing)
  Chalk and chalkboard (standing)
  Crayons on a large sheet of paper taped to the wall (standing)
  Shaving cream or talcum powder on a tabletop (sitting or standing)

Can You Picture This?

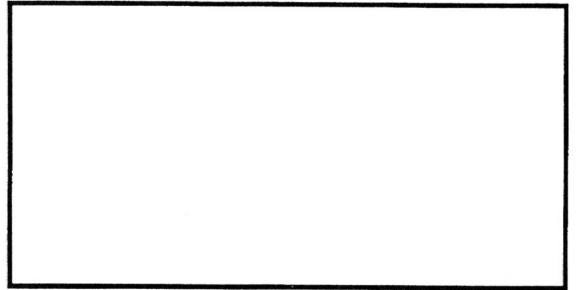

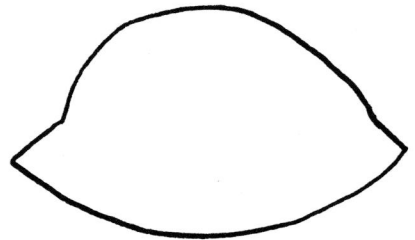

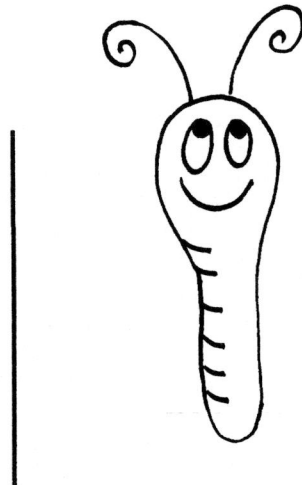

Activity 70: Shaping Up

Skill areas addressed

✔ visual motor skills, coloring, pencil grasp, in-hand manipulation, scissors skills and grasp

Goal

✔ The child will color and cut out the shapes with $1/4$" accuracy.

Supplies Needed

Photocopies of the "Shaping Up" worksheet

Washable, nontoxic markers

Child safety scissors

1 piece of construction paper (Allow the child to choose the color.)

Glue

Instructions

Present the worksheet and instruct the child to color in all the shapes. Encourage the child to go slowly and stay within the lines. Next instruct the child to cut out all the shapes, making sure the child's wrist stays in a position to maintain the thumb up while cutting. Finally have the child glue the shapes onto the construction paper in any desired pattern.

Suggested Modifications and Adaptations

- Demonstrate the activity if the child has difficulty understanding the directions.
- If the child has difficulty cutting and coloring with $1/4$" accuracy, provide extra practice or initial hand-over-hand assistance.

Activity 70: Shaping Up (cont.)

- Consult the OT for techniques to facilitate a correct scissors grasp and a tripod pencil grasp if the child is using an immature grasp for either. Also consult the OT if the child experiences significant difficulty or frustration completing the activity.

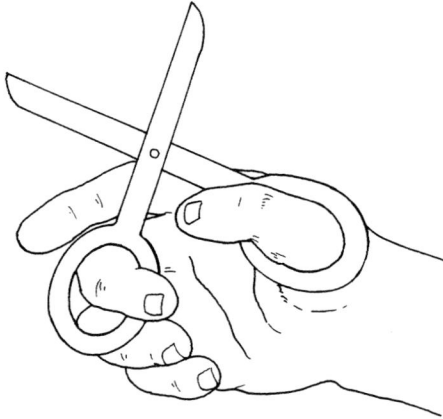

Correct, "thumb up" grasp   Immature, pronated grasp

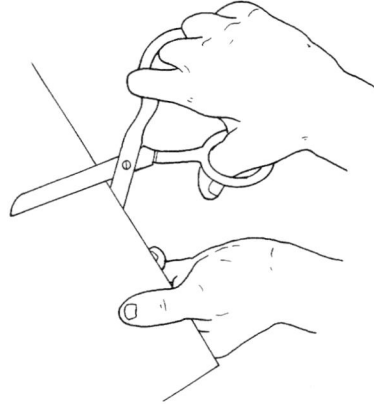

Optional Fine Motor or Educational Extension Activities

- Have the child choose a different color for each shape (e.g., making all the circles yellow, the squares red, etc.). Then once the shapes are cut apart, have the child sort and match them.
- Also encourage the child to count the shapes.
- Select other coloring, cutting and pasting activities from preschool activity books.

Shaping Up

 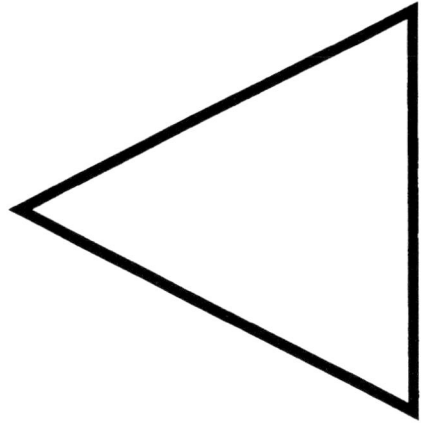

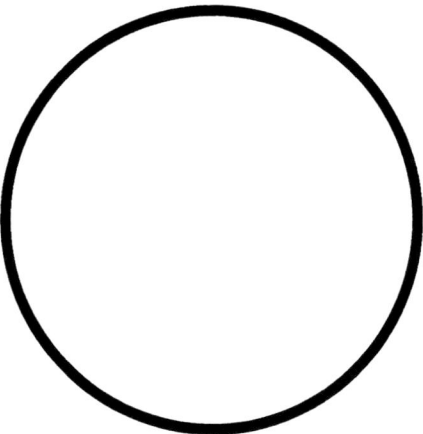 

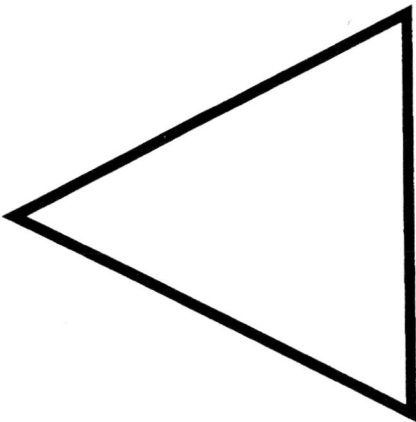 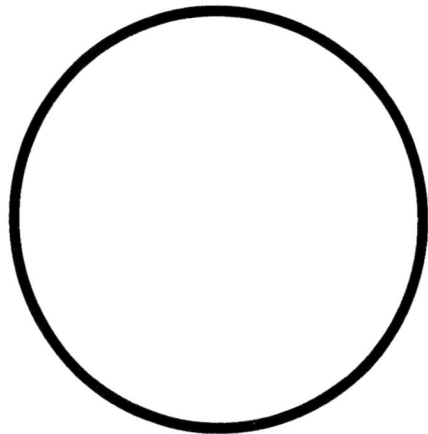

Glossary

Bilateral hand use involves grasping and manipulating objects with both hands. This includes activities in which one hand stabilizes the object while the other hand manipulates it. Examples of bilateral hand use include clapping, stringing beads and holding paper while coloring.

Copying involves seeing a completed shape (or letter) and drawing that shape (or letter). Also see *imitating.*

Dominant (preferred) hand is the hand that is generally larger, stronger and more coordinated. In common terms, people use the terms right-handed or left-handed. Hand dominance is established gradually during the preschool years. It is important to have the child use his or her best hand for these activities, so please consult with the OT to confirm each child's dominant hand prior to beginning this program. If the child has not yet established a dominant hand, please consult the OT to determine whether this program is appropriate and to find out techniques for assisting the child to establish a dominant hand.

Fine motor control, for the purposes of this program, refers only to those fine motor movements done with the hands.

Fine motor delay, for the purposes of this program, is a delay in using the hands and fingers and coordinating vision with these movements. Whether or not a child has a fine motor delay is determined by a trained examiner who administers a standardized developmental assessment of fine motor skills.

> *Mild fine motor delay* is defined in this program as a delay of one month to one year.

> *Moderate fine motor delay* is defined in this program as a delay of between one and two years.

Hand-over-hand assistance, for the purpose of this program, involves placing your (i.e., the facilitator's) hands directly over the child's hands and manipulating the child's hands to complete the fine motor activity. This allows the child to feel the actions required for the task. This strategy may not be effective with children who have tactile defensiveness (i.e., are hypersensitive to touch); consult the OT if you know or suspect that a child has this condition.

Imitating involves the student watching someone draw a shape or letter, then duplicating the shape (or letter). Whereas in copying the student sees only the finished product, in imitation, the student also watches how the shape is created.

Pencil grasp is used generically in this program to refer to grasping any writing implement. Markers are the writing implement of choice for this program. Also see *tripod grasp.*

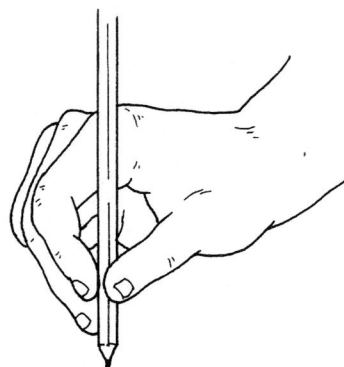

Proximal stability is defined within this program as stability with adequate strength in the shoulders and trunk musculature to allow for controlled distal fine motor movement (i.e., the arms and hands). Proximal stability should be determined by a trained examiner such as the consulting OT.

Scissors grasp refers to how the child holds and uses scissors. The thumb of the dominant hand is placed in the top loop and the third finger (or third and fourth fingers) is placed in the lower loop. The index finger is braced against the lower loop to give support. When first learning to use scissors, some children turn the wrist down (called pronating the wrist) so that the scissors are almost sideways to the paper. When the instructions read that the wrist should be maintained in a "thumb up" position, this indicates that the adult should discourage the child from pronating the wrist.

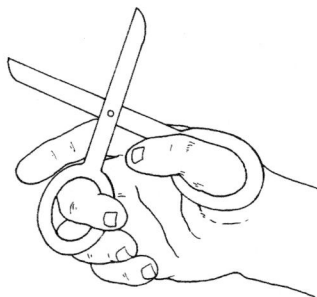

Correct, "thumb up" grasp   Immature, pronated grasp

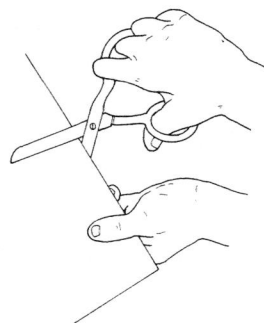

Tripod grasp refers to any of several forms of the mature grip used for holding paintbrushes and writing implements such as crayons, markers and pencils. The main feature of the tripod grasp is that the implement is held with the thumb and first two fingers of the dominant hand. (See "Overview of Motor Development," page 7, for more information.)

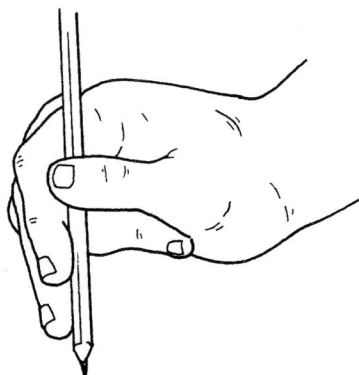

Lateral tripod grasp   Dynamic tripod grasp

Verbal cues are words or short descriptive phrases used to guide the child in completing a task or activity. For example, saying, "make a straight line, turn the corner, straight line, turn the corner. . . ." as you draw a square is giving verbal cues. In an activity with many steps, describe the first part of the procedure and allow the child to complete it, before giving the next step (rather than describing the entire sequence at once). This strategy may not be effective or may need to be modified for children with auditory processing difficulties (i.e., children whose hearing sensitivity is fine but who sometimes have difficulty understanding and remembering spoken words). Consult your OT or a speech-language pathologist if verbal cues seem to confuse rather than help the child.

Complete List of Supplies

All supplies needed to complete the numbered activities in the program are listed below. Supplies for the optional extension activities are not included.

Bags:	A large bag, preferably cloth, in which 10-12 small objects can be hidden
	Small paper lunch sacks
Beads:	12-15 medium beads ($1"$-$1\frac{1}{2}"$ in diameter) with a hole at least $\frac{1}{4}"$ in diameter
	10-12 small beads, approximately $\frac{1}{2}"$ in diameter with a hole $\frac{1}{8}"$ in diameter
Buttoning board:	Homemade or commercially manufactured buttoning board or vest with at least 3 buttons $\frac{3}{4}"$-$1\frac{1}{4}"$ in diameter (or use a shirt or jacket with $\frac{3}{4}"$ or larger buttons)
	Homemade or commercially manufactured buttoning board or vest with 3 or more $\frac{1}{2}"$ buttons (or use a shirt or jacket with $\frac{1}{2}"$ buttons)
Chalk:	Small pieces $\frac{1}{2}"$ in diameter and $2"$-$4"$ long), both white and colored
Chalkboard:	Vertically oriented—either easel-style or wall mounted—large enough for adult and child to work at simultaneously
Clothespins:	3 spring-loaded (rather than simply notched) clothespins
Cloths:	Damp cloths or paper towels for cleanup
Container:	A wastebasket or similar round container at least $12"$ in diameter for throwing crumpled paper balls into
	A container or marked area $5"$ x $5"$ for placing small objects in
Cotton balls:	10-15 cotton balls
Crayons:	Various colors, either preschool or regular size is fine

Drill:	A drill to make starter holes for screws
Egg carton:	A carton for 12 eggs, preferably paper rather than foam plastic
Glue:	White glue in a small bottle or glue stick
Hole punch:	A hand-held hole punch with handles that squeeze together (not one of the models that can be set on a table and pushed down with the palm of the hand)
Jars:	10-12 containers of various sizes with lids that screw on; for safety, plastic is recommended
Laminating supplies:	A supply of clear plastic shelf paper or laminating equipment
Markers:	Medium-sized, washable, nontoxic markers in a variety of colors
	Changeable markers (optional)
	Light-colored washable markers or highlighting markers
	Black permanent marker
Nuts and bolts:	8-12 bolts of different sizes, with nuts to fit, between $3/8"$ and $3/4"$ in diameter
Objects, various small:	15-17 small, lightweight objects that can be picked up with kitchen tongs, such as small toys, wooden blocks, Lego blocks
	10-12 small and distinct objects to fit in a grab bag: counting bear, clothespin, paper clip, safety pin, pen, marker, bolt, small block, small animals, pipe cleaner, crayon, etc.
Padlocks:	5-7 key-operated padlocks of various sizes, with keys to fit
Paintbrushes:	Brushes with thick shafts may be easier for children to hold
Painting smock:	A smock, old shirt or similar item to cover the child's clothing while painting

Paints:	Nontoxic finger-paints
	Nontoxic watercolor paints
Paper:	Sheets of tissue paper or newspaper no larger than 9" x 12", for crumpling into balls
	Paper to tear up, such as newspaper, tissue paper, construction paper or computer paper; ideally sheets no larger than 12" by 18"
	Construction paper ($8\frac{1}{2}$" x 11" or larger) in various colors, including black and white; use thick weights if available
	Strips of construction paper no wider than 1" and at least 5" in length
	Roll of butcher paper
	White and colored office paper ($8\frac{1}{2}$" x 11")
Pegboard:	A board that fits pegs $\frac{1}{2}$" in diameter, preferably made of foam
Pegs:	6-8 medium-sized pegs (the end placed into the board should be at least $\frac{1}{2}$" in diameter)
Pipe cleaners (optional):	Several colors to allow the child to choose a favorite
Playing cards:	Either a commercial memory card game, or any deck of cards with matching pairs of cards
Scissors:	Adult paper scissors
	Child safety scissors
Screwdriver:	A screwdriver small enough for the child to handle easily, with a head that fits whatever screws you use
Screws:	10-12 medium-sized wood screws
Snap board:	A commercially manufactured or homemade snap board or vest with at least 4 snaps (or any shirt, jacket, vest or pants with at least 4 snaps)

String or laces:	A string, with a hard tip, at least 12" long (A thin shoelace works well, or wrap the end in tape or dip in glue.)
	A string, with a hard tip, at least 20" long
	A string, with a hard tip, at least 40" long
	Long pieces of string for hanging paper art projects
Tagboard:	Strips of tagboard or thin cardboard no wider than $1/2$" and at least 5" in length
	Sheets of thin cardboard, tagboard or thick construction paper
Tape:	Masking tape to tape butcher paper to the wall or affix paper to an easel, or to mark off areas
	Clear plastic tape (optional) for wrapping string to make a hard tip
Tongs:	Lightweight kitchen tongs with handles that require active finger movement for both opening and closing (small enough for a child to handle easily)
Tube frosting:	A tube of frosting or squeeze bottle of ketchup small enough for a child to manage easily
Vertical writing surface:	Either butcher paper taped to a wall at the child's level or an easel
Water:	Small container of water for use with watercolors
Wood:	A block of soft to semi-hard wood for driving screws into, at least 5" x 5"
Worksheets:	Photocopies of all worksheets in this manual
Yarn:	5 or 6 24" strands of yarn

Bibliography

Beery, K. E., and Buktenica, N. A. *Developmental Test of Visual-Motor Integration.* Cleveland, OH: Modern Curriculum Press, 1989.

Benbow, M. Principles and practices of teaching handwriting. In Henderson, A. and Pehoski, C. (Eds.), *Hand Function in the Child: Foundations for Remediation,* pp. 255-281. St. Louis: Mosby, 1995.

Benbow, M., Hanft, B. and Marsh, D. Handwriting in the classroom: Improving written communication. In Royeen, C. B. (Ed.), *AOTA Self-Study Series: Classroom Applications for School-Based Practice,* pp. 1-59. Bethesda, MD: American Occupational Therapy Association, 1992.

Case-Smith, J. Efficacy of occupational therapy services related to hand skill development in preschool children. *Physical and Occupational Therapy in Pediatrics,* vol. 14, nos. 3-4: 31-57 (1995b).

Case-Smith, J. Fine motor outcomes in preschool children who receive occupational therapy services. *The American Journal of Occupational Therapy,* vol. 50, no. 1: 52-61 (1996).

Case-Smith, J. The effects of tactile defensiveness and tactile discrimination on in-hand manipulation. *American Journal of Occupational Therapy,* vol. 45, no. 9: 811-818 (1991).

Case-Smith, J. The relationships among sensorimotor components, fine motor skill, and functional performance in preschool children. *American Journal of Occupational Therapy,* vol. 49, no. 1: 645-651 (1995a).

Cornhill, H., and Case-Smith, J. Factors that relate to good and poor handwriting. *American Journal of Occupational Therapy,* vol. 50, no. 9: 732-739 (1996).

Cunningham-Amundson, S. J. Handwriting: Evaluation and intervention in school settings. In Case-Smith, J., and Pehoski, C. (Eds.), *Development of Hand Skills in the Child,* pp. 64-78. Bethesda, MD: American Occupational Therapy Association, 1992.

Davies, P. and Gavin, W. Comparison of individual and group/consultation treatment methods for preschool children with developmental delays. *The American Journal of Occupational Therapy,* vol. 48, no. 1: 155-161 (1994).

Dunn, W. A comparison of service provision models in school-based occupational therapy services: A pilot study. *Occupational Therapy Journal of Research,* vol. 10: 300-320 (1990).

Exner, C. E. Development of hand function. In Pratt, P. N., and Allen, A. S. (Eds.), *Occupational Therapy for Children,* 2d. ed., pp. 235-259. St. Louis: Mosby, 1989.

Exner, C. E. Development of hand skills. In Case-Smith, J., Allen, A. S., and Pratt, P. N. (Eds.), *Occupational Therapy for Children,* 3d. ed., pp. 268-306. St. Louis: Mosby, 1996.

Exner, C. E. In-hand manipulation skills. In Case-Smith, J., and Pehoski, C. (Eds.), *Development of Hand Skills in the Child,* pp. 35-46. Bethesda, MD: American Occupational Therapy Association, 1992.

Exner, C. E. In-hand manipulation skills in normal young children: A pilot study. *Occupational Therapy Practice,* vol. 1, no. 4: 63-72 (1990).

Exner, C. E. Remediation of hand skill problems in children. In Henderson, A., and Pehoski, C. (Eds.), *Hand Function in the Child: Foundations for Remediation,* pp. 197-222. St. Louis: Mosby, 1995.

Folio, R., and Fewell, R. *Peabody Developmental Motor Scales and Activity Cards.* Allen, TX: DLM Teaching Resources, 1983.

Haldy, M and Haack, L. *Making It Easy: Sensorimotor Activities at Home and School.* San Antonio, TX: Therapy Skill Builders, 1995.

Humphry, R., Jewell, K. and Rosenberger, R. C. Development of in-hand manipulation and relationship with activities. *American Journal of Occupational Therapy,* vol. 49, no. 8: 763-771 (1995).

Jewell, K., and Humphry, R. Reliability of an observation protocol of in-hand manipulation and functional skill development. *Physical and Occupational Therapy in Pediatrics,* vol. 13, no. 3: 67-81 (1993).

Kellegrew, D and Allen, D. Occupational therapy in full-inclusion classrooms: A case study from the Moorpark model. *The American Journal of Occupational Therapy,* vol. 50, no. 9: 718-724 (1996).

Kemmis, B and Dunn, W. Collaborative consultation: The efficacy of remedial and compensatory intervention in school contexts. *The American Journal of Occupational Therapy,* vol. 50, no. 9: 709-724 (1996).

Klein, M. D. *Pre-Scissor Skills* (3d. ed.). San Antonio, TX: Therapy Skill Builders, 1990a.

Klein, M. D. *Pre-Writing Skills* (Rev. ed.). San Antonio, TX: Therapy Skill Builders, 1990b.

Levine, K. J. *Development of Pre-writing and Scissors Skills: A Visual Analysis.* San Antonio, TX: Therapy Skill Builders, 1995.

Levine, K. J. *Fine Motor Dysfunction: Therapeutic Strategies in the Classroom.* San Antonio, TX: Therapy Skill Builders, 1991.

Pratt, P. N., and Allen, A. S., The role of occupational therapy in pediatrics. In Pratt, P. N., and Allen, A. S. (Eds.), *Occupational Therapy for Children,* 2d. ed., pp. 3-9. St. Louis: Mosby, 1989.

Rosenbloom, L., and Horton, M. E. The maturation of fine prehension in young children. *Developmental Medicine and Child Neurology,* vol. 13: 3-8 (1971).

Schneck, C. M. Comparison of pencil grip patterns in first graders with good and poor writing skills. *American Journal of Occupational Therapy,* vol. 45, no. 8: 701-706 (1991).

Schneck, C. M., and Battaglia, C. Developing scissors skills in young children. In Case-Smith, J., and Pehoski, C. (Eds.), *Development of Hand Skills in the Child,* pp. 79-89. Bethesda, MD: American Occupational Therapy Association, 1992.

Schneck, C. M., and Henderson, A. Descriptive analysis of the developmental progression of grip position for pencil and crayon control in nondysfunctional children. *American Journal of Occupational Therapy,* vol. 45, no. 10: 893-900 (1990).

Stephens, L. C., and Pratt, P. N. School work tasks and vocational readiness. In Pratt, P. N., and Allen, A. S. (Eds.), *Occupational Therapy for Children,* 2d. ed., pp. 311-334. St. Louis: Mosby, 1989.

Tseng, M. H., and Cermak, S. A. The influence of ergonomic factors and perceptual-motor abilities on handwriting performance. *American Journal of Occupational Therapy,* vol. 47, no. 10: 919-926 (1993).

Tseng, M. H., and Murray, E. A. Differences in perceptual motor measures in children with good and poor handwriting. *Occupational Therapy Journal of Research,* vol. 14, no. 1: 19-36 (1994).

Weil, M. J., and Cunningham-Amundson, S. J. Relationship between visuomotor and handwriting skills of children in kindergarten. *American Journal of Occupational Therapy,* vol. 48, no. 11: 982-988 (1994).

Wessel, K. E. *A Program to Improve Fine Motor Development in Kindergarten Children: A Practicum Report.* Fort Lauderdale, FL: Nova Southeastern University, 1988.

Ziviani, J. The development of graphomotor skills. In Henderson, A. H., and Pehoski, C. (Eds.), *Hand Function in the Child: Foundations for Remediation,* pp. 184-193. St. Louis: Mosby, 1995.

About the Author

Nory Marsh received the bachelor of science degree in occupational therapy from Colorado State University and the master of arts degree in education from Regis University. She has numerous years of experience in pediatrics and early childhood eduation. Currently she resides in Colorado, where she works as an occupational therapist in a variety of settings including private practice, home health and a local school district.